# THE SOUND OF THE BELLS

# ALSO BY JUSSI NIITTYVIITA

We Were Once Human
*A Definition of Transcendence*

Seeker of Silences
*Contemplations of a Silent Mind*

A Year of Stillness
*A Journey Into Inner Peace and Awakening*

I Forgive You
*An Unexpected Key to Awakening*

7 Days of Presence
*A Course in Inner Peace*

An Inquiry Into Reality

*More creations of peace and presence*

*available at www.jussiniittyviita.com*

# THE SOUND OF THE BELLS

BY JUSSI NIITTYVIITA

The greatest learning of the ages lies in

accepting life exactly as it comes to us.

- Anthony de Mello

# Contents

# About Stories and This Book

This book was originally intended to be published almost two years ago. However, when the first draft was practically ready, I was faced with a dire situation. A dear friend of mine, whom I appreciated very much, was diagnosed with cancer. He was one year younger than me, a respectable husband, and a loving father of two beautiful children. In January 2021, he passed away.

The arc of this particular personal story prevented me from writing quite much anything. Whenever I sat down to write, nothing would come out. When I even thought of writing anything or finishing this book, I felt an overwhelmingly strong resistance within me. During those two years, only some short texts were created, many of them as a product of pure willpower. I was practically forced to go within instead of pouring out. Then, one day in the autumn of 2021, as the days began to shorten and the nights grew rapidly colder here in Lapland, I was struck hard with spontaneous inspiration. In a very short time, this book went through some radical transformations. Now, as the book has reached its final form, I hold it as a tribute to my dear friend.

As I've come to understand, the curious pendulum-like phenomenon of going within and pouring out in turns is a common way for human beings to live their lives. We go within, we pour out, we go within, we pour out, and so on. Most people tend to be unconsciously afraid of going within. Therefore, they are compulsively pouring out—spending their time unceasingly doing, acting, reacting, and restlessly seeking some form of value and meaning from their lives. I know that going within is not always easy, and at first, there might not be anything of interest there.

After investigating this pendulum in my own experience, I can say without a doubt that going within, remaining there, and acting from within is one of the rarest and most beautiful jewels of wisdom. Constantly pouring out and living an active life without moments of silent contemplation is nothing compared to the magnificently alive stillness breathing within. If you give any sincere attention, you quickly find out that active life is usually a life of compulsion and reaction. Acting through a state of inner stillness—which is the same in you as it is in me—is not compulsive and reactive in any way. Instead, it's relaxed, compassionate, and accepting. Such a life is permanently fulfilling, a portrait of peace and presence.

From this fulfillment, action can pour out without resistance. I do not reveal this to set you forth on a journey to find any kind of gratification or fulfillment. You don't need a journey—you only need to turn within. The story I share with you in this book is my humble invitation for you to realize this.

The spiritual teacher Anthony de Mello once said: "A story is the shortest distance between a human being and truth." Stories are the most efficient tool human beings have ever invented to connect people with different truths. Additionally, stories exist to connect two human beings with each other. They minimize the distance one needs to travel to share ideas, beliefs, and values with someone else. This means, consequently, that stories minimize the distance between individuals in societies. After all, what is society and culture but a series of interactions between two individuals?

How *you* treat other people, what *you* say to them, how *you* react to their words or actions, is both the zenith of your society *and* the creator of it. *Your* everyday behavior is the culmination of your society—not the conclusion of it, but the ever-proceeding climax of its story. Your reactions are mostly based on stories that have shaped your sense of identity. In other words, your alignment to how you receive and how you give. Stories are the blood that runs through you and the veins of the society you live in.

Most stories, however, do not close the gap between a human being and truth. Instead, they are used as vehicles to meet myriads of ends. This may be done intentionally or unconsciously, but ultimately, it doesn't matter what purpose they hold hidden from your sight. A story that produces any kind of gratification or instant response is *not* a story that connects you with truth. Such a story connects you only with what you openly or secretly desire and what gives you a sense of temporary importance. Don't get these words wrong, though. Many stories that produce gratification can act as a bridge to become a better you, leading to better life situations. There's nothing wrong with that. Still, my aim here is simply to bring *awareness* to the stories that govern your life.

All stories are more or less transformational. The reason for this is that you are not a constant. You're a vortex in a river, through which water runs, and a whirlwind in the autumn winds, through which withered leaves fly. You're a flame, through which burning gases flow, and the soil, through which ten thousand plants grow. Every single thing you come across transforms you, whether it be a fictional story you read, a factual piece of science, a story someone tells you about herself, one you tell yourself about yourself, the social media feed you browse through, and even the news you read and watch in the public media. All of these different stories are intrinsically wired to change you or magnify what you already harbor within.

There are many kinds of stories told in the history of humanity. The ones I'm referring to from now on are *intentionally transformational.* It's a common word, yet its meaning is perhaps best explained by its Latin origins: *trans* meaning across or beyond, and *formare* meaning to form. Together, these words originally mean metamorphosis, a change in shape. For example, a caterpillar transforming into a butterfly is practically an embodiment of the word *transformation*. In the same way, people seek to transform, become someone else, and go beyond their present forms.

The common error you usually make when you come across a transformational story is that you instantly follow the urge to act on it. Usually, the action—or the *reaction*, to be more precise—aims for gratification directly or through seeking to avoid fear and suffering. That's perfectly fine, as long as you remain *aware* of your reactions.

How does awareness, then, bring anything to the table when talking about transformation? In my investigations of life and awareness, I've discovered that choiceless awareness of anything changes everything. If a story reactively compels you to commit actions and lures you into mental positions and opinions, it will push you away from truth. In that case, it is most likely that someone else's truth is forced into you through the medium of a story. You would do well if you learned to practice contemplation whenever you hear a story—either fictional or factual. Turn within, and ask: "Am I aware of what this particular story produces in me? What does its metaphoric nature mean to me here and now?"

Stories are *always* metaphoric, no matter how you look at them. Take, for example, one of the most famous stories of all time, the story of Jesus. Whether it is based on facts or fiction is not relevant. Instead, I'd encourage you to see the wisdom it has carried through a couple of thousand years—the wisdom which comes from understanding the metaphor. Your ability to contemplate the metaphoric nature of Jesus' story in general, as well as the smaller parables within it, will make a crucial difference. Profound wisdom is expressed every time you can remain with a story, *be* with the story, and look from within the story instead of reactively forming mental positions around it.

This book is full of stories and parables that, over the years, have tuned awareness on my part to the correct channel—the present moment awareness. Even the very basic idea this book expands on is a short parable named *The Temple Bells*, one I've heard from Anthony de Mello. Some stories and parables presented in these pages you might recognize, and some might be entirely new to you. While reading, keep in mind that this story is metaphoric in every angle you look at it. Even the book's name introduces a metaphor that I believe will dawn on you no later than when you close the last page.

I wish you a contemplative time reading *The Sound of the Bells*. Remember to stay aware. Stay present. Be an island of sanity in a world full of confusion.

With you here and now,

Jussi Niittyviita
23rd of October 2021
Ylläs, Lapland, Finland

# The Invitation

This time, the dream was intense. He knew he was dreaming, but the mysterious scenery was too compelling for him to even want to wake up. The Unnamed in him loved the dream beyond understanding. A strong pull into the unknown mystery was constantly inviting him ever deeper. He would have followed the pull without blinking an eye if there wasn't an equally strong resistance within. He was in a state of a total paradox, reflected in the dreamscape in front of him.

There was an island, an ocean, and a storm. The storm was unlike any he had ever witnessed. Winds blew with terrible intensity, and enormous cresting waves met the island's shores with majestic force. The darkness embracing the island was lit by an intricate dance of lightning. Despite the raging storm, he could feel serenity emanating from the waving ocean. He couldn't figure out what created this peculiar sense of peace, but it definitely gave meaning to the storm winds. It was this strange stillness in the raging ocean that the Unnamed within him longed for. The immense gusts of wind penetrated his ethereal body, and the roars of thunder cracked open the whole dream-reality. Despite the storm's ferocity, he felt safer clinging to the storm than approaching the Unnamed's tempting whispers.

A temple stood on the solitary island. There were a thousand bells in the temple, both big and small, crafted with immeasurable skill and precision. As the storm winds blew, the bells pealed out in unison, creating a symphony of an overwhelming balance of sounds. It was perfection, plain and simple, continuing for an undefined time without beginning or ending. He knew there had never been a time when he had *not* heard the symphony, and he knew there could never be such time. He witnessed a symphony that echoed in all eternity.

Then, he started falling. He plunged through the cresting surface of the ocean toward the bottomless darkness below. Slowly and steadily, the surface above moved further away from him. The whirlwinds of furious energies and flashes of lightning became only distant perceptions in the corner of his eye. The island was gone, the temple was gone, and the storm was gone. Still, he could hear the bells pealing out their magical symphony in the unknown depths of the ocean. It was now loud and clear, without any interference from the storm winds and roars of lightning.

Like an uninvited guest, panic started to infiltrate his mind. He realized how tiny a fragment he was in the ocean, embraced by infinite masses of water and endless depths of unknowable blackness. An urge to inhale grew stronger moment by moment. He craved to get back to the surface where he could breathe with the storm winds and witness the violent flashes of lightning. Yet, at the same time, the symphony of the bells was sending his whole being into raptures. The Unnamed within him was home with the stillness of the symphony and depths of the ocean.

The urge to inhale became unbearable.

Breathing would mean the end of him.

He chose to breathe.


Michael was afraid to open his eyes as he lay sweaty in his bed. Trembling, he took a deep breath and slowly opened one eye to see if the storm was really gone. The bleak ceiling of the hospital's room was steadily in place and greeted him with a silent 'good morning' just like many times before. For a short moment, Michael was certain that he could still hear the bells, but when he tried to listen more closely, all he could hear was silence and his slowly steading rhythm of breathing. The dream had occurred every night since the surgery, but it was very different and alive this night. Now, it felt like more of an invitation.

Michael felt gently assured by the intense pounding of his heart. The old trusted machine beating in his chest brought about such simple peace he had never known before. He could not hear the bells anymore, but a silent clarity had fallen down on him. His thoughts were crystal clear. He knew what had to be done.

One week had passed since the doctors had told him the words that would steer the rest of his life: "Michael, we're sorry. You have three months to go, at best," they had said. Many other things were also said, but most of it was covered with blurry memories and a hazy rollercoaster of emotions. He was now slowly recovering from the surgery, which had given him the extra three months' time.

The impact of those heavy words had struck him down hard. His life wasn't supposed to go like this. Most importantly, it wasn't supposed to *end* like this—withering silently in a bleak hospital room. He was 'Michael, the business emperor', a successful entrepreneur who had the most wonderful life by the standards of modern society. He had a busy schedule, a vast network of friends and acquaintances, money, and resources beyond imagination. He had big plans and a calendar full of important meetings that would literally slingshot his company up into the interstellar space. Michael was a success, as people would always say—few with admiration and many with jealousy, or that's what he had always thought was lingering behind people's eyes.

Michael had unconsciously taken the phone in his hand after waking up from the dream. He remained motionless, staring at the black screen. His whole life stared back at him from the blackness with empty eyes and depressing silence. A shudder went through his body. The short moment of peace that had followed the dream was already gone. He let the phone drop to his side on the hospital's bed, relaxed his head on the pillow, and took a deep breath. A lonely tear ran down his cheek.

Michael couldn't bear the idea of telling of his situation to friends and colleagues. What terrified him even more was that he had no one he would *first* tell of his surgery and condition. A wave of loneliness washed over him. For a fleeting moment, the whole room felt threatening. Michael closed his eyes and yearned to get back to the dream. He tried to listen to the symphony of the mysterious bells. Still, he could hear only the silent whispers of his own loneliness.

Some subtle rays of the sun penetrated the window blinds. The lifeless white wall of the hospital's room was painted with an unmoving dance of light and shadow. It felt strange and discouraging that he would not see such dance anymore after three months, more or less. His life was about to end. 'Michael' was about to be no more.

"Good morning. How are you feeling today?" The nurse came in, carrying a tray of breakfast. "Any pain or discomfort?"

Michael tried to smile and quietly shook his head. He thought the nurse must have seen through his forced smile. It took a significant effort to hide the bottomless loneliness that had just unfolded within. During the years in business, he had grown accustomed to concealing his feelings and wearing the 'Michael-mask', as Jason would sometimes say. Thinking of Jason elevated his mood a little, even though he was just a colleague and not a friend.

Michael slowly rose up to sit at the bedside and examined the breakfast.

"Nice one today. Thanks," he said and forced a smile again.

"The chefs were on fire this morning." The nurse smiled back at him with a compassionate look in her eyes. Maybe the compassion was really there, or perhaps it was just Michael's imagination, something that he wanted to see—needed to see.

"It's going to be alright. I know you're feeling down at the moment, but you'll get better for a while now. You'll have the strength to put things in order. But don't procrastinate. Time is not on your side," the nurse said quietly, walked to the window, and opened the blinds. For a short moment, the whole room bathed in blinding light before Michael's eyes adapted. She turned back to face him with the familiar compassionate look on her face. "Just buzz if you need anything. There shouldn't be any pain from the surgery now, but if there is, the doctor must take a closer look at you."

*Time is not on my side*, the echoes of the fateful words whirled in his head as the nurse walked away. "Time..." he whispered and could taste the bitter word in his mouth. Time had always been on his side. It had been his closest friend on the way to glory and fame. Time and his skill of timing were the most pivotal reasons for his success. But now, time had left him alone and deserted in a small hospital room. Michael felt nauseous, unable to touch the breakfast. Silently, he lay down on the bed. Even though waves of loneliness and anxiety came and went, the dream returned to him as a warm memory. It was the memory that finally steered his hands to grab the phone again.

"Hi, Jason," Michael said immediately as Jason answered the call. He did it on purpose to keep control of the call to himself. "I've been invited. Don't ask where or why, but this is an invitation I can't decline. I'm gonna be away for a long time, and I'll make sure the board will have you selected as the CEO for now."

"Uh," was all Jason could say after a short and confused silence. This wasn't like him at all. Jason was usually the one who was always talking and would have the quickest answer to everything. However, the bomb Michael just dropped seemed too much for him. Then he cleared his throat. "Mikey, what's going on? First, you take a week of vacation, which you haven't done like forever, and then you tell me this? Has something happened? Is everything ok?"

"I've had surgery," Michael responded quickly to get back on track with his own thoughts and plans. "The doctors say I have three months to go at most. But that's not the important thing here. What's important is what I just told you."

"Fuck you, man!" Jason breathed out, using language Michael had never heard him use. Then after an awkward short silence, Jason whispered. "Is it really terminal? What is it? Cancer? Something else? I'm sure you can afford the best of the best to treat whatever it is. Don't just take their word for it, but instead, fight. Michael, you need to fight."

"Jason, I've already got the best of the best treating me. They're the ones who gave me the three months extra. Now listen closely," Michael said and improved his posture. "You need not know what the illness is. You need not know what has caused it. You need not know anything about my condition, and I would appreciate it if you didn't tell people about this. Time is not on my side now, and I feel I'm already running late for my invitation. I'll handle the board to have you take my place. It shouldn't be too hard. I believe they like you much more than they ever liked me."

"Invitation? What are you talking about? You can't do this. Isn't it against some laws? Shouldn't you handle some stuff you've got going before doing this?" Jason was clearly perplexed.

"I can do it, and I will. The empire is yours. Take good care of it. Take good care of yourself. I must go now. Maybe I'll contact you later." Michael hasted to end the call as tears swelled up in his eyes.

The memory of the dream literally pushed him to abandon everything that made him the man he was—his business empire and all things connected to it. The decision was hard, but he had no other option choose, which made the decision quick. The feeling of being invited echoed in the remnants of the dream. He was left with no alternatives but to follow the invitation. For some reason, Michael knew when and where, but nothing very exact. He slowly stood up, gathered his belongings, and prepared for the last journey of his life.

# The Old Man and the Tree

The morning sun slowly appeared from beyond the horizon. The first golden rays painted the whole world with yellow light and reflected a shining bridge on the gently waving ocean. A light wind was blowing, and the distinct smell of the sea embraced the whole shore.

Michael stood on the rocky beach motionless, watching the sunrise with mixed feelings. On the other hand, the scenery's beauty invited him to relax and come closer, but anxiety and loneliness still penetrated his being like thousand swords. He felt disoriented and didn't have the slightest idea why he was doing what he was doing. *Maybe I should have taken care of my empire until the end, instead of journeying to this god-forsaken remote village,* the thought returned to him frequently in different words and mental images.

A strong urge to call Jason flowed through him once in a while. However, Michael resisted the urge with pure willpower because somewhere within him, the invitation still echoed its mysterious and silent words. His mind tempted him to get back to the life of 'Michael' for even just a few more months, but his heart encouraged him to follow the invitation.

Michael didn't know why he had become so obsessed with Jason over the past few days. He was never a close friend, maybe not even a friend at all. Jason was a colleague, and that was all. Of course, the man had been supportive. Without him, Michael's business empire would not have blossomed the way it did. Still, their relationship didn't quite fulfill the requirements Michael thought friendship would have. After reflecting on his own thoughts, a curious idea was starting to take form in his mind. Jason inhabited now Michael's role as the CEO and frontman of the companies. *Jason was 'Michael' now.* Shivers went down through Michael's spine. He shrugged the feeling off, took a deep breath and braced his posture.

It had been seven days since he had left the hospital. Leaving had been somewhat difficult since the doctors had insisted he stayed a few days to ensure full healing from the surgery. Nevertheless, he had left, disregarding all professional objections. He had gone straight to the airport without even dropping by at home. The idea of visiting home was absurd because dead men had no homes. Home meant nothing to him. Michael, the business emperor, was now homeless, a derelict. Of course, he still had his money, but little did he need to use it. It seemed that as life was about the reach an endpoint, material interests and personal ambitions faded quickly away. The meaning of time was profoundly changed. Before, his every thought was concerned with all kinds of futures, and now, time was a quickly diminishing frame constricting the portrait of his remaining life. That realization caused some additional suffering, and Michael knew it was suffering he had to bear through his remaining days.

The journey to the village had been complicated and not so comfortable. After a long flight, he had endured a few hours of extraordinarily noisy train and a painfully long and uncomfortable bus ride. Michael had followed his intuition about the invitation, but he had no idea why come to this exact village. Still, it felt right for him. The Unnamed within him had accepted the invitation, guided him through the journey, and was now satisfied with the place he was in.

Michael had found a small cabin in the village's outskirts. The cabin was located next to a path that led to a nearby mountain, which dominated the landscape with its majestic presence. He rented the cabin for a relatively low price, and the price was quickly proved correct. It smelled strange inside. One of the small bathroom's walls was covered with mold. In the dead of night, he could hear some disturbing rustle every once in a while. Whenever he put the lights on, some cockroaches hasted to safety into the dark corners of the room. The cabin had electricity, but Michael didn't know what to do with it, other than have the lights on. He didn't even need to charge his phone because the dead phone alleviated his longing to reach back into his past life.

There were approximately five hundred people in the village, more or less. The first glance revealed quite a poor lifestyle. The modern living standards had obviously not reached this part of the Earth yet. It wasn't middle ages, but definitely not 21st century. Still, there was something peculiarly peaceful in how the villagers lived. They woke up just before the break of dawn, prepared for a new day with the early morning sun, spent their time heeding the weather and occasionally working—not to gain great fortunes, but fulfilling their individual functions in their small society.

Being in the village felt strangely paradoxical. Michael would have had the money to buy the whole village countless times. Still, there he was, living like a man spending his last possessions and riding the wave of destiny for a reason he didn't know. He felt huge uncertainty with the whole situation, amplified by his dire physical condition. Yet, he was deeply assured this was the place and time meant for him. Here and now.

He took a deep breath of the light sea breeze and strolled slowly along the rocky shore. Some fishermen in the distance were preparing their old boats for the morning's fishing trip. Sounds of the villagers starting a new day filled the air, but it was nothing like the constant background noise of the big city Michael was used to.

Here, the noise was absent. There was but silence, occasional sounds of the villagers, and the rustle of his footsteps on the beach rocks.

He walked on the shore without a destination for half an hour and arrived at a curious-looking place. Some coconut trees were growing near the water in a small verdant area. Their shades created an inviting shelter from the quickly rising morning sun. He took a sip from the water bottle. The villagers' occasional noises faded away far behind as he walked forward, and only the subtle sound of the waves on the shore remained. Otherwise, it was plain silence. Michael felt a spontaneous glimpse of peace for the first time probably in many years. Too many years. The silence of the coconut trees seemed to absorb all the anxious thoughts that had steered his emotions for the last few weeks.

He stared at the gently waving ocean embraced with a subtle serenity. A tear rolled down his cheek. Michael wiped it away quickly as if someone was looking and judging him. He was raised to believe that real men don't cry. He could almost hear his father's voice telling him so. As he lowered his hand, a familiar thought appeared. *What am I doing here? I should call Jason and tell him I'm coming back.* Michael tried to shrug off the thought with a deep breath, but to no avail.

"You seem to have come a long way, stranger," a distant voice interrupted the beginning of the too-familiar thought pattern.

Michael hesitated. He wasn't sure if someone had really spoken, or if it was just his imagination. He really had come a long way, abandoning his remaining life for just a dream. Silence fell down on him once again, followed by the distant feeling of peace. He glanced around. It seemed that he was alone. Maybe it really was his own imagination doing tricks on this crazy journey.

"Forgot how to speak, or do you go by some other language than English?" the same distant voice threw a question, filling the silence with a strange distinction.

"Oh, I do. I do speak English," Michael answered, not sure which direction he should face. The shades of the coconut trees caught his attention after a short moment. A shadowy figure was sitting motionless under one of the biggest trees. Michael didn't know what else to say. So, he decided to continue with a small compliment as he approached the huge tree. "A very nice place you've got here. Peaceful."

"Peaceful, yes," the voice replied, now a bit closer. "But it's not mine. It would be absurd for anyone to own this kind of peace."

Michael was still a bit confused about the situation and just walked until he reached the tree and the shadowy figure. An old man was sitting under the tree motionless, like a statue. His eyes were locked in the ocean, or maybe the horizon. He made no effort to encounter Michael face to face. The old man's face was covered in wrinkles that framed his whole presence with a strange harmony. It seemed as if the old man was growing from the same roots as the coconut tree he was leaning back on. A delicate smile rose on the old man's face as Michael stepped next to him.

"I guess that you heard the bells?" The old man kept staring over the sea. His voice was a bit hoarse, but the words were spoken with a steady and slow rhythm that reflected his motionless being.

Michael's heart stopped for a fleeting moment. How could this man know about his dream? Was this the reason he had come to this remote corner of the Earth? The confusion grew deeper, and all Michael could do was to bluntly stare at the old man.

"The bells are pealing out all the time," the old man continued, with the smile still on his face. "However, not many are willing to hear their symphony. Only a few are really willing to listen to it..." The old man paused for a moment. The smile withered from his face, revealing something expressionless. "...and very rarely it happens that someone starts dancing with the symphony. Not always, but usually, the dance starts after a personal tragedy, after enough suffering is present in one's life. Say, stranger, what story does your suffering tell?"

The question hit like a sharp sword through Michael's state of confusion. "I'm going to die in three months," he answered without even thinking about what he should say.

"Everything is dying all the time." The smile came back to the old man's face even wider than before. It made the wrinkles in his face bend and deepen into a natural-looking expression. "We all know this, of course, but it seems to me that you can feel it. It's a totally different thing to wake up in the morning and *feel* like a man who might die than to just know it. Let me ask you a question," the old man paused again for a moment as if he intentionally sought to emphasize the question. "Are you alive here and now?"

"Still alive," Michael sighed. "But as I said, time is not on my side."

"Are you just saying that you're alive? Or can you feel it? Not just knowing it, but really *feel* it, in the same way that you feel you are going to die?" The man turned his posture for the first time to face Michael and looked deep into his eyes.

When their eyes met, something in Michael's mind turned upside down. For a tiny fraction of time, which was not supposed to be on his side, he felt time disappear. The mindset that produced the answer 'still alive' just a few moments ago was gone. It was replaced by a peculiar sense of emptiness, where he could actually *feel* the aliveness in his body. Before the sensation could continue any further, a flood of thoughts came pouring in.

"Still. Alive," Michael emphasized what he had just said, and felt a grain of irritation within. He turned to face the gently waving sea to hide his emotions. *Who is this stranger to ask me such questions? Maybe I should call Jason and discuss my remaining months*, he thought. Michael would definitely have some ideas to make the empire's future more glorious, even with himself out of the picture. The previous sense of emptiness was quickly replaced by a sense of importance. He felt safe in its familiar embrace. He had always been important. Why shouldn't he be so even after death?

"You're drifting off, stranger." The old man smiled as if he was reading Michael's thoughts. "What's your name?"

"Michael," Michael said and glanced at the old man, unsure if it was wise to share anything with this man. "Michael Ward."

"Michael, what you say or know has very little meaning. If you threw yourself in the middle of that ocean and fearfully screamed to yourself, 'I'm drowning!', your words would not actually reflect what you're feeling at the moment. Instead, they would represent your fear of drowning. Now, fear is actually just a future you think you have. In the same way, when you say, 'still alive', you're expressing automation dictated by your past. You've been alive for quite many years now, so you don't have to give it any attention.

"The problem is, that if you speak words without giving attention to reality, your words will end up being soulless echoes in the minds of men. Did you know, Michael, that attention is the currency of love?" The old man chuckled quietly as if he was amused by his own words. "Attention is the middleman in the seemingly complex arrangement of your life and the world."

There was some distant wisdom in the words that Michael could not quite reach. If he had heard such words just a few months ago, he would have judged it as complete nonsense. After all, words had built his business from scratch to an empire. Without words, it wouldn't have been possible. But now, in this strange place, in this odd discussion with an unknown stranger, he just let the words sink in for a while.

"So, you're saying words are redundant? Just soulless echoes? I seem to have achieved quite much using words as my tools. You wouldn't even know." Despite appreciating the old man's words, Michael followed his sudden inner urge to undermine them. He didn't even mean to do so, but the words came out as a habit. After all, his work in modern society had been about winning in the game of comparison. That game intrinsically included an aspect of undermining. It had all been a game of inferiority and superiority.

"We are witnessing the vanity of the human mind here. But don't worry, Michael, we all must wade through vanity for the simple reason that we are human beings." The old man kept smiling at him with a compassionate look in his eyes. "The vanity is that your mind can see only black and white. Somewhere deep down within, you think black is the one and only truth, and therefore, for you, white cannot be true. And vice versa, if you think white will win the game of life, then black must be shoved away.

"When dealing with words, your reasoning is always filled with loopholes. Information can be shared through words, but it's impossible to share the clarity of experience. Words are soulless echoes, indeed, but only if they lack pure and unjudging attention. Luckily, we all have the ability to give such attention. Only a few of us align with it, though. The ability to give attention is your birthright and what you already naturally do. The attention is yours to give away—you cannot keep it to yourself. So far, you haven't been very conscious of using your birthright. The focus of your attention constantly drifts from one place to another. We are here to fix this together. That's why the bells brought you here."

"How do you know about my dream?" Michael had almost forgotten the old man's previous reference to the bells. Then he added cautiously. "Is it some group hallucination, or something like that?"

The old man burst into genuine laughter. "Yes, Michael. It is indeed a group hallucination! You put it quite right there."

"Oh," Michael said, smiling at his own question, and partly because the old man's laughter felt contagious. "I didn't mean to put it that way, but I guess it must be that then. I traveled across the planet to a god-forsaken village because of a group hallucination. Good for you, Michael."

"Group hallucination it is. Maybe, if the stars are aligned correctly, and the goddess of good luck smiles upon you, you will someday truly see this hallucination." The old man changed his posture a bit and stared once again to the distant horizon. "But you will need attention for this good luck to happen. Full attention. Relentless attention. Michael, you spoke of achievements just a few minutes ago. What do you think achievement is? How would you define success?"

"Success, for me, is the accomplishment of an aim and purpose. And all the things that derive from this accomplishment—for example, a big mansion as a home, a dozen flashy cars in the garage, a vast network of friends, fame, recognition, and money—form the climax of success. I guess success is best defined through them," Michael spouted out without thinking any further. As soon as the words came out of his mouth, they felt empty. What did all those things mean to him now that he was going to depart from the world in a painfully short time? A wave of anxiety washed over him, but it was quickly dispelled by the old man's steady voice.

"Say you have those things, but every night when you go to bed, is your sleep affected by the size of your mansion? Can you drive all those flashy cars at the same time? Where are your friends when you drift off to sleep? How about fame and recognition? Worst of all, those things caused you to lose your peace of mind, and you fall asleep with a stained conscience. Would they mean anything to you then?" the old man asked, and Michael already knew the answer from personal experience. All the things he had achieved, had caused him to lose his peace of mind, each in their own way. After a short silence, the old man affirmed his own words. "Maybe true success is a paradigm shift in human consciousness, which leads to peace of mind and crystal-clear conscience."

Those words left Michael unarmed. He had experienced painfully well what the modern society standards and business life would do to the ones seeking success. Even though his achievements were high on every meter of society, they had rarely brought him fulfillment. And those that did, the fulfillment didn't last very long. As a young man, he had always believed that money would solve all his problems, but how wrong he had been then. As Michael had made his first millions, he had faced a gruesome paradox. When he was still poor, he imagined that being rich would bring him lasting happiness, but when he got rich, he began to long for the simple life he had when he was poor. So, he did the only thing he knew, and it was to find something seemingly greater to achieve.

"Oh," Michael sighed silently and gazed at the waves arriving slowly to shore. On this remote rocky shore, he now saw clearly the rat race he had trodden all his life on. It wasn't meaningless to him at all, but he realized that he was never quite fulfilled in that race. He had never had peace of mind and crystal-clear conscience the old man talked about.

"It's all about attention, Michael," the old man said silently with a warm tone. "Be fully aware of where your focus goes, lest life takes you to places that are not quite true—illusory pleasures and empty promises of fulfillment, also known as 'sufferings'. Relentless, pure, and unjudging attention will save you from suffering. And I would suggest you start with the very basic things you can give your attention to. Things that are a tiny bit more real than what you've just described as a success. For example, your body. Feel the heart beating in your chest. If it didn't do that, you wouldn't be here wondering about money and other achievements. Smell the ocean breeze as it comes from unknown journeys from the distant horizons. Listen to the birds sing as they begin their morning fishing ritual over the surface. Feel the rocks under your feet when you tread on this rugged shore."

The old man stopped abruptly. He took a few deep breaths as if he was smelling the damp air the ocean brought with it. The wide smile was back on his wrinkled face. The old man seemed like an embodiment of peace sitting there, leaning back on the coconut tree's trunk.

"Michael, give attention to your breath. When you draw a deep breath, be aware that you draw a deep breath. When you draw a shallow breath, be aware that you draw a shallow breath. And what do you do when you draw a medium-sized breath? Be aware, aware, and aware. Still, keep in mind that watching your breath is just a beginning, an analogy. Breathing is the essence of the world around you. Every single thing is in constant exchange with its surroundings. Nothing can be truthfully defined without being aware of the vast environment also. Opposites depend on each other. Black wouldn't be black if there were not white. They are intrinsically interconnected so that the essence of white is actually black. To see this, the awareness of breathing—the constant interconnectedness of things—must be there at every turn of your life. The flame of awareness must burn bright within you.

"However, don't understand this wrong. You need no effort for this. Giving attention should be effortless. Otherwise, it would not be giving attention, but more like craving for attention. You need to get out of your own way." The old man drew one deep breath again and glanced at a bird gliding near the water's surface. "Look how they fly—no effort at all. If you look very closely, you'll realize that the birds do not fly, but they ride the winds. In the same way, fish do no swim, but they are carried by the water. They express their essential nature in the movement through their environments. You cannot define a fish without water, or a bird without the winds. To see this effortlessly, you need choiceless attention, which, by the way, is very close to *your* essential nature."

"I must say I'm confused. I never thought that a dream would bring me here. Yet, here I am," Michael whispered, mostly to himself. He stared at the bird making tight turns in the air and occasionally diving deep under the surface. "Oh, I must be going. My landlord is expecting me in half an hour."

"Ride the winds, Michael. Ride the winds." The smile had not dissolved from the old man's face for a single moment during the last part of their conversation.

"Hey, by the way, I didn't get your name?" Michael asked when he was about to leave.

"Names can name nothing that lasts. They are not important. But for the time being, you can call me…" The old man paused for a moment like he was trying to make up something from thin air. "…Old Man. Yes, you can call me Old Man. I suppose it describes me best at the moment."

"You do bear the resemblance of an old man." Michael gave a short laugh. "But yeah, we've got a deal. I'll call you Old Man for the time being."

Old Man returned to his noble silence and gazed at the horizon once again. Michael strolled back to the direction where he had come from and turned to glance at the coconut tree grove in the distance. He could see a solitary figure of a man, sitting motionless under one of the trees. Strange peace emanated from the distant sight. The peace accompanied Michael the whole way back to the cabin.

# THE COCONUT TREE GROVE

An increasing level of anxiety was taking hold of Michael's days. For a couple of weeks, he strolled every morning on the rocky shore, hoping he would find Old Man in the coconut tree grove, but time and again, his hopes proved empty. Sometimes he repeated the walk during the day. This particular morning he was unsure if he even wanted to meet Old Man there. The memory of the encounter was pleasant, but it was powerfully replaced by the idea of the approaching death. Maybe Old Man was just false hope in his time of suffering.

The night had been restless. All the thoughts about his life and the business empire had whirled through his mind, keeping him awake most of the night. In the morning, some minor pain was present in the stomach, reminding him of his worsening physical condition. Michael laid in his bed for a long time before getting up.

He plugged the charger in the dead phone and placed it on the notebook laying on the bedside table. Plans formed in his mind how he could get back home, but the memory of home left his soul barren and hollow. He unplugged the charger with an angry gesture.

The dream had not occurred even once after the vivid experience in the hospital. Its absence made Michael frustrated, and the feeling fed the anger and anxiety in him. *We are here to fix this together. That's why the bells brought you here.* Old Man's words echoed in his head, full of empty promises. Here he was, in this remote village with nothing to hope for and nothing to gain. He was following empty promises that had already faded long ago with the ocean breeze. *How could I be so naive?* Michael thought as he summoned some strength to get out of bed. *How could I let myself believe any of this? Time is not on my side here. Time is really not on my side.*

He found himself standing on the front porch with a water bottle in his hand, just like many mornings before. The pain in the stomach had alleviated a bit. Still, the pain was there to remind him of its presence, like a looming shadow of the nearby mountain over the bright morning. Michael pulled himself together and started walking. He decided to go through the village's town square on the way to the beach. His landlord had told him that every morning, one could buy fresh fish from the fish market. He wasn't hungry, but needed some social contact, even though most people in the village didn't speak English.

Other people's presence made most of the dark thoughts and feelings temporarily subside.

The people in the village were courteous and seemed quite happy. They smiled and greeted Michael in their own language. He had already learned how to say 'good morning', or that's what he assumed the words meant. The smell of the fish in the market was intense. Michael was relieved that the ocean brought some light wind that replaced the smell even for fleeting moments. Everywhere he looked, he saw people smiling, even though the conditions were very poor. He also noticed that the smiles were contagious. Michael found himself responding with a smile at a few people when passing their fish booths. He wasn't used to smiling at people he didn't know, at least when just passing by. In the big city, such behavior wasn't very ordinary—people were always busy to get from one place to another, and everyone was always restlessly moving and doing something. There had never been time to smile at strangers in the city.

There were a couple of shops in the remote corner of the fishmarket—a small grocery store and even a smaller cigarette store. *Maybe food and cigarettes are the only things that a human being really needs*, Michael found himself amusedly thinking. He had noticed that quite a many people smoked cigarettes in the village. He wasn't used to such sights because in the big city, people were quite aware of the health issues of smoking. He decided to pay no interest in the shops for now, and continued walking.

The fish market was left quickly behind as he arrived at the rocky beach. For a moment, he paused to breathe the refreshing air the winds carried from over the sea. The morning sun had already warmed the rocks under his bare feet. It felt peculiarly pleasant to just stand there for a while. The light breeze, the breath, the stones, and the pain in the stomach transformed something within him. Michael realized that even though his head had been full of thoughts and emotions, there had been a terrifying emptiness within him. Surprisingly, this very moment on the beach with those few little things seemed to fill his empty vessel with subtle and unconditional satisfaction.

*Attention*, Michael thought. *Hell, Old Man might have been on to something with all his talking.* He noticed the feeling of anxiety subsiding again, just as it did at the fish market with all those exchanged smiles. The ominous feeling didn't disappear completely, yet he felt relieved that he didn't have to do anything about it. Anxiety was there as a part of his experience, just like the breath, the breeze, and the rocks.

He strolled along the rocky beach slowly, giving attention to every single step he took. Walking started to feel more satisfying the more he gave attention to it. As satisfaction increased, he became aware of the absence of noise around him. The world had calmed down. His ears were resting in plain silence. No background noises from the village, no chirping of the birds, and no sounds of the waves. Only his own breath and his footsteps were present. Satisfaction started to slowly turn to peacefulness.

By the time he arrived at the coconut tree grove, his state of peace was incomparable to what he had ever felt before. It wasn't powerful or very distinct, but its subtlety made the experience magnificent. The stillness of the surrounding world had brought upon a stillness within. In that stillness, there was no room for thoughts of any kind. He approached the trees and was delighted to see a familiar-looking figure under the same tree once again.

"Surprised to see an old man so far from the town here." Michael smiled as he stepped next to Old Man. "It's been a while."

"Michael, what do you think of that tree there?" Old Man pointed to a tree a few meters from where he was sitting. "Maybe if you sit down this time? I guess a dying man doesn't need to hurry anywhere anymore?"

"Yeah," Michael sighed, sensing a soft fragrance of the familiar anxiety again. He disregarded the feeling quickly and went by the tree. He shoved the tree lightly with his hand. It felt sturdy and stable. Then he sat down and leaned his back against the tree's trunk, just like Old Man did. "I'm in no hurry this time."

The following few hours were something Michael had never experienced. Neither of them said a word but only gazed at the still ocean in front of them. Very little happened during the morning. Occasionally, Michael felt an urge to get up, and go check if the fish market was still there, or maybe get back to his cabin to make some food, but the urge diminished very quickly. Any wandering thought was absorbed by the peculiar silence on the beach.

Michael had not been so still for as long as he could even remember. He had lived a life of movement and purpose. In such a life, there was no space for stopping because everything needed to be put in order. Michael had been raised to think that to 'make it' in modern society, things constantly needed to get done. Now, under the coconut tree's shade on the rocky beach, he didn't even know what it meant to 'make it'. They were just empty words echoing in an empty valley. Instead, the newly found silence was so intriguing he could have listened to it forever.

"Attention," Michael said with a silent voice. "Giving attention is the way to silence, isn't it?"

"It is, Michael. It is indeed," Old Man responded after a short moment. "I'm not surprised you found it out yourself. Anyone who spends his time giving even a little earnest attention to *what is* will find silence within. It is a gateless gateway to inner peace. And where there's no gate, there's no division. You see, inner peace is already here and now. You just have to be aware of what is. Don't try to change what is because it changes by itself in time. Instead, just see, listen, taste, smell, and feel whatever sensations there are. Experience fully whatever you experience here and now.

"Your life is a river running through different lands. There might be lands that give you pleasure. There might be regions that fuel physical pain and mental suffering. Be aware and find appreciation toward the world around you. Then, inner peace will flow. Yet, you cannot obtain this inner peace by trying to attain it. You can't make the river still with force. Awareness and giving attention will bring this inner peace to you. And what do you think this peace is that I'm talking about?"

"I guess it's silence," Michael answered before he could even think about it. "At least, silence is what I'm hearing at the moment."

"You're quick to learn, Michael." Old Man glanced at him, with the familiar wide smile on his face. "Sometimes the silence will come through the openings inside your own mind. For example, seeping through the fabric of the knowledge that you're going to die. Sometimes it comes through the openings in the world around you—silent places, like this beach today. External silence gives you the possibility to hear inner silence. And inner silence is practically the same as inner peace. It cannot be attained, but you can become aware of it. The peace I'm talking about cannot be owned by anyone. Yet, it is within the grasp of everyone in this funny little group hallucination."

A long silence followed. No words were spoken. The sun journeyed across the sky, and the coconut trees' shadows shifted slowly in the opposite direction across the beach. The weather was unexpectedly still. Even the shadow spots had turned hot under the scorching sun.

"Michael, some years ago, I was told a fascinating story," Old Man broke the silence abruptly. "There once was a man who had lived his whole life near a mountain. One day he decided that he would climb to the top of the mountain to see what the world looked like. He packed some gear and went on his way. At the foot of the mountain, he encountered a traveler coming down from the peak. 'Greetings, traveler. What's the road like up to the summit? How are the views up there?' the man asked the traveler. The answer was simply: 'The terrain is rough and difficult, and it was too cloudy to see anything while I was up there.'

"The man decided to find another way to the top. After journeying some distance on the foot of the mountain, he encountered another traveler, from whom he asked the same questions. This time, the answer was: 'There were quite a many travelers on the path, so if you want to go by yourself, you shouldn't take this route. The views on top of the mountain were ok.' The man decided to take another route, and another, and another. Many travelers he met who had visited the top of the mountain. After hearing them all, the man had heard enough and decided he would not have to climb the mountain. He went back home, believing he knew what it was like on the mountaintop.

"You see, Michael, words can be full of images, each one more beautiful or appalling than the other. If you take anyone's words for anything as the truth, you will miss the clarity of self-gained knowledge." Old Man chuckled quietly as if there was something funny in his words. "Would you really know anything about honey if someone described you its myriad attributes? Honey tastes sweet. It's soft and sticky and colored yellow. It can be used as a remedy for some digestive ailments. You could read on thousands of pages of information about honey, but would you know anything about it that was real?

"One of the most destructive children of men is ignorance. Where ignorance roams, there cannot be peace. And where there's no peace, there's no silence, and thoughts are running wild and confused. The only way you can have self-gained knowledge is to be aware of your surroundings without preconceived ideas. Not knowing is the way to liberation. You can know honey only if you have seen it, tasted it, smelled it, touched it, and yes, even listened to it. You can know what the view is like on the top of the mountain only if you have traveled there yourself. Don't mistake anyone's words for truth, no matter how factual or scientifically proven they might sound. Because words create just noise in the peace of silence.

"During your life, you have met and will meet countless travelers coming down from their mountains. Each one of them is trying to force their own truth into you. Some travelers have seen God up there. Others have seen science and facts. Some have taken the spiritual path, and others vow in the name of materialism. One has felt the aliveness of the world and another has seen a dead and mechanical Universe. They come down from the mountaintop, selling their own black or white. They tell fascinating stories of the path they took. All those travelers are unconsciously trying to define *you* through their own words, and unless you stand guard at the gates of your mind, you will be defined by them. You already have countless times. Every path you have taken has already been described by a traveler that went and returned before you.

"Still, none of those paths have taken you to the mountaintop. You have yet a truth to discover. You still have a mountain to climb. And remember, truth does not reside in the land woven with paths. Truth is like valley streams—it runs silent and in shadows—and you don't recognize it until you've seen it through a totally different perspective. *Your* perspective."

"A good story," Michael uttered, sunken deep into his past. "I guess I have let too many people get under my skin. Maybe the doctors' news of my condition was just the peak of the iceberg. You know, Old Man, it really gets to you when someone insists on telling you as the truth that you're going to die in three months. It has this overpowering effect on your thoughts and emotions. It really tips the balance off and leaves you unguarded. Uncertain. Unsafe."

"Words have magical effects. Of course, there are situations where words are really beneficial. Still, if they make anyone feel uncertain and unsafe, they are placed horribly wrong. Such words are fueled by the destructive child of man—ignorance—no matter how much facts they are backed up with." Old Man coughed a few times, cleared his throat, and continued with a hoarse voice. "It would do you good always to reflect on your thoughts, whether they are based on self-gained knowledge, or knowledge someone has forced into you. I call these deep knowledge and surface knowledge. Like this vast surface of the ocean in front of us, surface knowledge is made of constantly changing waves. The nature of surface knowledge is highly ephemeral and forgetful. Deep underneath the waves, majestic stillness moves, producing deep knowledge. Deep knowledge is *who you are*. You know it even in silence. It may take time to realize that, but after you have access to deep knowledge, you will find out that you don't need time. So, the saying 'time is not on my side' is actually just a surface phenomenon that rises and falls like the ocean waves."

Silence fell down on the coconut tree grove. The still surface of the ocean mirrored the rays of the sun. The ocean floor was visible as far as the eyes could see. Near the shore, the ocean floor was paved with dark grey rock, but further away, it turned into white sand imprinted with the wave patterns of the water. The immensely clear water was a reflection of the silence in the grove.

Michael felt confused. Yet, at the same time, his thoughts were embraced by strange compassion. *Three months to live and time is not on my side*, Michael thought. *This is nothing other than mere surface knowledge. Have I ever stopped to examine how three months feel like? What does 'time' feel like?* The only thing Michael could sense about his looming death was that he was alive now. And counterintuitively, the surface knowledge gave even more meaning to the inevitable fact that he was alive. His 'three months to live' shifted to the appreciation of being alive now. In a blink of an eye, his perception changed. Time-bound fear turned into love of just existing in silence.

"Beware, Michael, of becoming a traveler yourself, selling your truth to others. Truth cannot be forced into anyone—it can only be found. You shouldn't take even my words for granted. Words cannot liberate you from your suffering. However, what I speak of, that most people are not aware of, and are not even ready to hear, are things that *point* to your truth. Instead of using your words to sell your truth, use them to guide. Don't cling to my words. Find out what lies at the end of the pathless path my words are guiding you on. And that pathless land you must travel in silence, lest the aberrations of surface knowledge mess up your journey," Old Man whispered the last words, and Michael could barely hear them. "Michael, listen to this coconut tree grove. Can you hear it? The trees whisper silent words of the love of being. Even when storm winds blow, those same words echo here with the same impeccable subtle power. They bear the essence of silence within.

"Silence is an essential aspect of all forms, thoughts, and things. Most of the time, you are so immersed in streams of thought that you overlook silence. Giving attention to the silence within is one of the brightest stars that will guide you to your truth. Your peace. No matter what storm winds blow, the silence is there within your awareness. Just look for it, and you'll get to be the man on the mountaintop."

"How do I know, then, when I have found this pathless land?" Michael hesitated, overwhelmed with a totally new perspective. "Are there signs to ensure I'm on the right track? If there even is a right track in this trackless land of yours."

"Michael, the land is not mine. Beware of the words you use. Your words are molded by your beliefs, just as your beliefs are affected by your words. They both are highly vague and ephemeral. Choose your words wisely," Old Man said slowly. "And no, there are no signs other than the absence of your present thoughts. A wise man once said: 'The Kingdom of Heaven doesn't come with signs to be observed.' This is what I'm also talking about. You will know you are on the mountaintop when no more signs tell you how to reach the mountaintop. All the signposts that lead to the summit shine with their absence."

Michael felt a small sting of anger. Old Man had some wise words, but he blatantly underestimated Michael's understanding. Of course, he knew how his mind worked and what effects his words had. Everyone knew how beliefs shaped the world. *Everyone.* And this ragged old man seemed to think that he, Michael the business emperor, had no clue of the power of beliefs. A distant shadow of hate arose in the wake of anger. He was unsure if he wanted to come again to meet with Old Man.

"Your mind needs you confined in chains," Old Man continued, seemingly unaware of Michael's silent outburst of feelings. "Give the mind anticipation and plans, and it will respond 'yes'. Give it problems and anxiety, and it will respond 'yes'. 'Yes' to all mental images of joy and sorrow, love and hate, hope and fear, pride and shame, desire and disgust. 'Yes' to all feelings of inferiority and superiority. But ask it to be silent, and it will say 'no'. The mind will never let you have your freedom. Still, only silence is where your freedom is found. This is the fall of man. This is the dilemma number one, a circumstance to be solved before anything else can be effectively solved. Nothing can be truly solved without a healthy state of detachment from the mind. A silent mind is a creative mind. The more compulsive thoughts and emotions you harbor in your mind, the more stagnant it becomes. Simply give attention to the silence within. Then, you might find yourself standing on the mountaintop."

Michael was still battling within with the feeling of being insulted by Old Man's words. The idea that he would not come again to the coconut tree grove demanded more space in his mind. *I wonder how Jason is doing*, Michael thought. *Maybe I should call Jason and let the man know the plans I have for the empire. Perhaps I should travel back home and take care of the last things properly. I did not come here chasing empty promises of a dream just to be insulted by a stranger.*

"Michael, I'm glad that we will meet again here in quite a short time. At dusk, our destinies will cross once again." Old Man looked at Michael and smiled compassionately.

Michael's mind stopped. It felt like a lightbulb was just lit in a darkened room. He became aware of his feelings of anger and hate. *'It's a totally different thing to wake up in the morning and feel like a man who might die than to know it.'* Old Man's words from the past echoed in the emptiness of his head. It's a totally different thing to *know* how beliefs work and *feel* how they work. Michael realized that he had just become the victim of his own mind when the feelings of anger and hate arose. He had not felt how his intellectual arrogance led to a feeling of being insulted, even though his thoughts had been flocking around the very same subject.

A wide smile decorated the dying man's face when he strolled back to his simple cabin in silence.

# The Dusk

Two weeks had gone by without a glimpse of Old Man on the beach. Each evening, before the sun disappeared beyond the horizon, Michael walked to the coconut tree grove. He sat there in silence and alone, leaned back on the same tree, watched the beautiful orange-hued rays of the setting sun, breathed the clean ocean breeze, and listened to the sounds of the waves. On a few occasions, he remembered the dream and tried to listen if he could catch the symphony of the bells, but to no avail. The dream was, after all, just a dream.

The coconut tree grove had become his safe haven—a sanctuary of inner peace and contentment. Otherwise, Michael's daily life was a rollercoaster of emotions. Sometimes he dwelled in a peaceful stillness of inner silence. Still, such moments passed quickly by only to be replaced by the too-familiar anxiety. A distressing throbbing pain in the stomach that came and went like the ocean waves didn't make it any easier to cultivate inner peace. Michael counted that if the doctors' predictions of his condition were correct, he would have less than two months left. The thought of it weighed his mood down. The loneliness he felt in the remote village amplified the feeling.

The villagers were as hospitable as ever. Michael had learned a few new words to handle the most basic things in the fish market. The ritual of buying some fish had become the most common communication for him. Sometimes it felt easy and natural to respond to the villagers' sincere smiles. At other times, when dark thoughts had their chains on him, his smiles were forced and soulless. Nevertheless, he had decided to wear a mask of politeness and succeeded seemingly well in doing so.

Many times, he walked past the cigarette shop in the fishmarket, simply out of curiosity. So many villagers smoked cigarettes that there had to be something the shopkeeper did right. However, everytime he walked past the shop, it was closed. The curiosity subsided after a while, and his usual walking routes changed to the far side of the fishmarket.

Despite his varying physical condition and the spectrum of feelings, he repeated the same routines every day—a morning walk to the fish market, a midday walk to the nearby docks, an afternoon nap after chatting with his landlord, who happened to speak English as fluently as he smoked cigarettes, and an evening walk to the coconut tree grove. Michael had always been a man of routines. He vowed in the name of adopting beneficial habits on his way to success and fame. He couldn't come up with any reasons why he should abandon his routines, even with the looming shadow of death growing bigger each day. After all, it was reasonable to approach the unwanted with good habits.

Dusk painted the horizon with bright orange and red hues, and the sun was about to touch the edge of the horizon. Michael watched two birds playing in the air. Their swift race took them close to the trees at times, only to carry them toward the setting sun until only two small dots could be seen in the distance. They flew back and forth, occasionally disappearing behind the coconut trees, only to appear some distance away again. Their complex yet effortless play colored the whole evening with a growing wonder in Michael's heart.

"When a song of a bird breaks the silence of the sea, watch closely, and you will see the dancer in the waves," the familiar hoarse voice said behind Michael. He had not heard Old Man coming. "It's a local saying. The villagers have some peculiar traditions here."

"Aren't you one of them?" Michael smiled and felt a warm sensation in his chest as he turned to face Old Man. "One of the villagers, I mean."

"My roots are elsewhere. Far from here. But it's not important," Old Man answered shortly as he sat down on his spot. "Do you know why they encourage to watch closely? Because the song of the bird gives meaning to the silence, and only in becoming aware of the silence can you truly see the dancer. And what a beautiful dance she has."

"I came at dusk like you said. I'm glad that I'm here," Michael said after a moment of silence as the birds made a quick turn of direction over the grove. "The past two weeks have been—how should I say it—frustrating. Every time I come here to sit in silence, I need and desire nothing. But my life catches me while I'm in the village. Maybe it's the presence of other people that draws my mind toward the rollercoaster of emotions. Sometimes I feel peaceful. Life flows like a valley stream—silently and by itself—but I think my condition is worsening. The pain is more dominant than before. I don't feel like eating most of the days. I don't feel like doing anything because what's the point. I've two months left. I'm a dead man walking. Then, occasionally, this mood of depression changes to soothing stillness. A strange sensation of peace covers the whole world. Though, the depression always tends to linger way longer than the peace."

"Life is a reflection of pleasure and pain." Old Man chuckled in his habitual manner as if something that Michael said was funny. "Accept them both. Enjoy them. Let them go. Dance like you owned them all, and maybe the dancer will show herself to you."

Michael didn't quite get the statement. He quickly ceased to figure it out, waiting for a follow-up, an explanation for the dancer. But Old Man kept noble silence, just gazing at the horizon and the setting sun. Michael tried to shrug off the confusion. *A dead man walking,* his mind echoed the thought a few times before merging with the setting sun into the silence.

"So, Michael, the dead man, has become a seeker of silences. That's good." Old Man broke the silence. "Sometimes death can bring great relief. A looming death disarms you of your delusional feelings of importance. Knowledge of the approaching end forces your mind to prioritize things again. In that great reorganization of the mind, many things will be relinquished. Your identity consists solely of those things that are let go of, and a soothing emptiness and feelings of peace are likely to emerge. Search within yourself, and you will find that is what's happening to you at the moment.

"The old 'Michael' disappears from time to time when the mind truly faces its own end. This is what reveals the moments of peace you described. Then again, the mind is mechanical, and it likes to find the old tracks quite often. The mind is not ready to let go of its self-made identity. This is what you suffer in the moments of your depression. Now, here comes something highly beneficial. Accept your pain just like you accept your peace. Acceptance is the source of all happiness, and awareness is the heart of acceptance. Accepting your highs and lows becomes natural when you're aware. So, do not resist pain and do not turn away from it. That's what the mind reactively does unless the great rays of awareness illuminate the makings of the mind."

"I'm still not sure if I can ever enjoy pain, neither physical nor mental. It feels wrong even to think about it."

Michael noticed that the sky had been empty for a while now. The birds' race had taken them to distant horizons. Their absence brought forth a stronger sensation of inner peace. "How can you enjoy pain? Why should you accept suffering?"

"Oh, you shouldn't enjoy suffering. Mostly because it is not real. Only something that appears as suffering exists, and it takes place in your mind. I'm not trying to turn you into a masochist. Self-flagellation, both physical and mental, leads only to ignorance. The joy does not come from the things that give you pain and suffering. The joy comes from being aware of your pain and suffering. No greater joy exists than being aware. Or maybe I should put the words differently: *being awareness*. Awareness is always present. It shines through all your thoughts about who you are and what you experience." Old Man stretched his legs and shifted his posture a bit. The wrinkles in his face were deep in the dim orange light of the setting sun. He seemed even more merged with his coconut tree than ever before.

"I can tell you that being aware is not a virtue of an average human being." Michael chuckled and gazed at the last rays of the sun before it disappeared entirely beyond the horizon.

"Being aware has nothing to do with being virtuous. It is not a question of ability. If you harbor any idea of virtue, you are not aware—you are confined in your own idea of virtue. True virtue does not emerge with virtuous intention. True virtue emerges naturally and spontaneously as a reflection of who you truly are.

Awareness of that reflection makes space for acceptance, and acceptance introduces gratitude. This arrangement fuels miracles. This cosmic dance is impregnated with true virtue. The only way you can feel apart from the dance is your idea of separation, which arises in your mind. I said 'feel apart' because you cannot really 'be apart' from this dance. You *are* awareness whether you like it or not and whether you remember it or not. Awareness is asleep in an average human. Yet, what is asleep is bound to awaken. *You* are bound to awaken." Old Man turned to look at Michael with the familiar wide smile on his face. His smile was simultaneously compassionate and loving, yet playful and even a bit mischievous.

"So, we should all become seekers of silences sooner than later?" Michael wasn't sure where the conversation was going. He just flowed with Old Man's words toward the darkness of the night.

"Yes and no." Old Man replied quickly. "Becoming a seeker of silences is a trap, which you actually have already fallen into. You've experienced the silence and peace, as you described before. This means you want it. You wanting it returned is an indication that you've started seeking it. However, as long as there's a seeker, silence will not truly unfold. What you seek you cannot have here and now, mostly because you're seeking from the wrong places. You're seeking inner peace from your ideas of where and how to find it. Thoughts will never allow you peace. They will lead you astray into endless forests of ignorance. Despite this, seeking is a crucial part of waking up. You just have to seek from the right place. Turn within, Michael. Turn within.

”Seek the true silences and not the empty promises of your mind. Put your trust in the process of seeking instead of finding, and you will find out that when the search is over, the seeker has disappeared. This can happen here and now. The search is practically already over. You just have to let go of all your pleasures and pains. Let them be and enjoy being just awareness. It is not easy—it's easier than easy. It's so simple that the human mind cannot grasp it. Therefore, for the mind-made identity, any true awakening is impossible. Your mind thinks you must add something to yourself to attain lasting inner peace, but how wrong it is. Perfection is attained only when everything unessential is relinquished. And you don't have to do or become anything to let go. This is the beauty and sacredness of the present moment—the power of the Sacred Moment.”

Michael remained silent, contemplating the words blossoming with strange wisdom. His state of peace had turned into a state of wonder. The beauty of the last rays of the sun touched the coconut tree grove from behind the horizon. Tears swelled in his eyes. All his life, he had been led astray, and it had taken death itself to wake him up from the dream of endless chasing of gratification. Many remnants of that delusional dream were persistently surfacing, resulting in waves of myriad emotions of which most were dark and depressing. Leaning back on his coconut tree, Michael saw his life as a whole and knew he needed to add nothing to who he was.

"Your desire to awaken is not personal, Michael. You are not alone," Old Man whispered as if he had read Michael's thoughts. "It's a movement, like a wave in the ocean. A wave doesn't decide where it will go next—it is bound to follow the ocean's course. This doesn't mean that you are without a choice, flowing toward some predecided destiny. I mean that your awakening is not your choice. The existence wants to awaken, Michael, and you're part of it. You are it, just like the wave is part of the ocean. There's nothing you can do about it. If you resist, you will face doctors saying that you'll die in three months. You will meet many other travelers also that will try to shake you awake—some with gentle words and some with brutal force. Let go of your resistance. Accept that you are something the whole existence is doing. Awakening is a universal movement."

"I suppose there's still some resistance in me, even though I'd like to think otherwise. Maybe my inner resistance is the reason for the waves of darkness I've experienced lately," Michael said and felt a lonely tear fall down his cheek. "I've seen that my mind plays tricks with me all the time. How, then, can I find out if there's resistance in me?"

"One day in the distant past, a warrior came into this village. He was feeling down, just like you sometimes— worried, depressed, regretful, and on that very day he was a bit ill-tempered also. He wasn't always like that, but that day he had gone through a lot." Old Man nodded a few times as if to approve his own words and continued. "Yes. A lot had he taken that day. But he was lucky. Some of the villagers told him there was a holy man, who knew the secrets of life itself, living in the village. The warrior raced to meet the holy man. When he found the man, he spoke up: 'Holy man, I need guidance. I've gone through many pains and sufferings lately, and my self-confidence is down. Can you tell me the difference between Heaven and Hell?'"

The holy man looked at the warrior with contempt in his eyes and responded: 'Why should I share such a secret with a man like you? That secret is for the wise only and is meant to be heard only by the good men. Obviously, everyone can tell that you are not among the wise or the good. You seem despicable and a failure as a warrior. Warriors need self-confidence, which you clearly lack. You would do best to put your sword down here and now, and go live your life among the beggars who are more of your kin.'"

The warrior was outraged by the holy man's words and unsheathed his sword. He was deeply hurt and felt raging anger lift its head. The warrior prepared his whole body for a mighty strike. In the crucial moment, just before the sword would have cut down to end the irreverent insult, the holy man turned his face toward the warrior and smiled compassionately. The warrior lowered his sword, bedazzled and confused. The holy man said: 'This is Hell. You are possessed by your darkest emotions.' A sense of humility and remorse washed over the warrior. The holy man had risked his own life to give the answer. He kneeled before the holy man, realizing the lesson he had just learned. 'Holy man, please forgive me. My hand will never rise up again, led by my dark emotions. I will live my life by the highest of emotions and unparalleled standards of love and compassion.' The warrior felt ashamed and made a silent vow to himself. The holy man smiled and replied compassionately: 'And this, my beloved warrior, is Heaven. Soon, peace and serenity will embrace you.' Then the holy man kneeled in front of the warrior, and they both bowed sincerely to each other before parting."

The sun had already disappeared entirely. Its last rays were engulfed by the rising darkness of the night. Old Man's words seemed to echo in the air for a while. Then, silence fell down on Michael. Silence, unlike anything else before. Deep peace and serenity embraced him in that silence. He didn't know what to say or do, so he humbly lowered his head as if bowing to the fading image of the holy man in the story. Tears were now flowing without resistance. One by one, they dripped slowly to the ground. For the first time, which felt like forever, Michael felt truly and unconditionally happy. He was content.

"There's resistance in you when you're engulfed by the darkest of emotions. And yes, even a tiny bit of irritation is a reflection of resistance. Even the smallest grain of resistance has the potential to tip the balance of peace and carve a hole in your heart. So, harbor nothing negative within you. Let it go as soon as you become aware of it. That is the power of awareness and the promise of the Sacred Moment," Old Man said silently. Michael couldn't see his face, but he could sense Old Man's compassionate smile. "Accept the Hell around you and within you. Accept the misfortune, illness, and misery that may knock on your or your loved ones' door. Accept the poverty, the famine, the wars, and the epidemic that might shake humanity. This does not mean that acceptance is a vow of doing nothing. Acceptance does not equal passivity.

"Still, remember never to lift your hand up led by the darkest of your emotions. Without awareness and acceptance, you will breed more darkness with your blind reactions. Accept your Hell, and you will remember Heaven. There's an old saying by an ancient swordsman: 'Under the sword lifted high, there is Hell making you tremble. But go ahead, and you have the land of bliss.'"

Again, deep silence fell down on the coconut tree grove. He had experienced many aspects of silence in his time in the village and sometimes he thought there was nothing else to it than the serenity it produced. Still, the silence somehow succeeded in deepening every time he felt it. It was always different. Always pure and pristine, and without form. Michael could not help but feel a wordless wonder. Somehow, his state of wonder seemed to deepen the silence and give an indistinct meaning to it.

The last rays of the sun waned beyond the horizon. The late evening became darker with every heartbeat. The pale light of the rising moon lit up the ocean's gently waving surface. Stars painted the skyline with their distant glimmer. The coconut tree grove seemed like a totally different place in the darkness. The silent and colorless trees sought solace in the steady ground, and the treetops reached for the distant lights of the stars. The trees seemed as if they were exhaling after a long inhale. It was their time to relax after the day in the scorching sun.

"Michael, my beloved warrior," Old Man broke the silence with his hoarse and whispering voice. "You would do well if you realized one simple thing: darkness can only exist because of light. They co-create one another, just like silence is the only thing that gives meaning to sounds. When the sun sets and the darkness of night falls down on you, remember that it's only because light exists. In your darkest moments, embraced by the darkest of emotions, just let the darkness be and exhale. Look directly at the darkness, and you will see it is filled with a glorious light of silence. Darkness is nothing but emptiness. Seek not to fill it with your thoughts. See how everything connects in a mutual arising. Light and darkness, the colors and colorless, the forms and formless. Listen to the sound of the balance of everything. Taste it. Feel it. This balance is true silence. Don't interfere with the balance, accept all sides of it, be grateful for it. Bless it.

"Your awareness is the sacred blade that will cut through all empty illusions. And whenever you find yourself under a sword lifted high, you will see how the raised sword has created an opening, a way through, if you're but ready to see. The world is filled with swords lifted high, Michael. All kinds of darkness and personal

Hells present themselves to you. Still, there are just as many openings to the land of bliss, which is yours to reclaim. Inhale when it's time to inhale and exhale when it's time to exhale—feel the rhythm of life as waves arriving at the shore. Feel the crests and the troughs. Feel the Sacred Moment and how it guides your every step on your path to the mountain."

Then, Old Man let the silence of night sink in again. His words echoed in Michael's mind like a distant shout in an empty valley. The words brought forth an even greater experience of wonder. The silence was deep and again deep.

# THE MOUNTAIN

Michael was feeling a lot better most of the time. Anxiety and darkness came and went, like the ocean brought its waves to the shore—constantly and relentlessly. He had realized that the waves were the whole ocean's second nature. The realization made his emotions feel mostly like temporary surface phenomena, with strange stillness underlying it all. With the waves of anxiety came also memories. At times he was perplexed by the memory of the dream that had brought him to the village. The remembrance of the bells always produced some wordless frustration. He had not even realized how much he wanted to hear the magnificent symphony of those thousand bells again.

Sometimes, on his long walks along the rocky shore, he would cultivate the silence within. Inner silence always revealed some peace from beyond the waves of anxiety. However, the silence never lasted for long. Michael had taken as routine to go for a walk whenever his personal Hell would raise its head. Sometimes he found himself walking on the shore under the starry sky in the middle of the night, after dark thoughts had shaken him from sleep. During such nights, he tried to hear the bells even harder. The absence of their symphony empowered his frustration. The harder he tried, the brighter the frustration burnt. At such times, he allowed himself to exhale, just like Old Man had said. Then, he wandered resolutely back to the cabin through the darkness of night.

As his mental condition was getting better, the pain in the stomach was increasing. Some days he could feel it only as a distant throbbing. On other days it was more evident. Occasionally, he had to take some painkillers to fend it off. However, the strong medicine balanced its benefits with strong nausea. He didn't eat at all on such days. Even drinking water felt like a forced habit. During those dark times, he felt the familiar urge to grab his phone that had laid lifeless on the bedside table the whole time he'd been in the village. He longed for the idea to call Jason. He needed to control the empire once again, even for a short moment before fading away into the unwanted. Michael also played with the alluring idea of proper care in the hospital on his last days. Still, for a reason he knew not, it didn't feel the right thing to do.

On one day, as the first rays of the sun shined through the closed curtains, Michael decided he would take another kind of a walk. A solitary and small mountain dominated the landscape in the outskirts of the village. He had lived his whole life in smaller or bigger cities and had never climbed a mountain. Not even a small one like this. Michael estimated it would take him some hours to reach the mountaintop in his deteriorated physical condition, and hoped that the pain would not creep in that day.

Michael woke up and changed a few words with the landlord about the mountain. With a half-burned cigarette hanging from his mouth, the man told there were two ways to climb it—the hard way, of course, and an easier path on the southern side of the mountain.

"It's been called the Craven's Path since I was a little boy. There's a solitary signpost on the south side showing you the way," the man said, amused, but admitted that if Michael had no rock climbing experience, that would be the proper path to take. For a fleeting moment, Michael considered taking the hard way contrary to the landlord's recommendation. Maybe he could get some distance up. Then, his feet would slip, and he would tumble down the steep side of the mountain. His life would end quickly with a broken spine and a cracked skull, instead of withering slowly and painfully. Michael played with the thought for some time. Quickly it subsided, and the Craven's Path felt a wiser option.

He packed two water bottles, a loaf of bread, and some painkillers in his backpack. After pondering a while on the cabin's small porch whether it was a good idea at all to climb a mountain in his physical condition, he decided it was something he had to do, even if it was his last thing.

Michael, the dying man, would climb to the mountaintop. He would see for himself what the views were like up there.

The small and curvy path, which led to the mountain's southern side, took him about an hour. The walk felt easy and effortless. Soon, he arrived at a crossroads. It was evident which way he should continue. Just like the landlord had said, someone had taken the liberty to place a poorly constructed signpost with worn scribbles. It was written with the local language which Michael couldn't read. Yet, it was obvious the signpost was labeled 'The Craven's Path', since Michael had not seen any other signposts on the way there. By its ancient looks, whoever put the signpost there would already have been deceased or at least arrived at a considerable age.

Michael took a sip of water, put his cap firmly on his head for protection from the scorching sun. Decisively, he continued on the mountain path. During the first hour of climbing up the gently sloping path, many thoughts stormed through his head. At times he would think of the words of Old Man with warmth. Some memories of Jason and his empire surfaced. Subtle worry of his looming death arose in his mind. All thoughts came and went, and were eventually replaced by a monotonous habit of counting steps. Michael's mind wouldn't allow him the peace that he so often experienced on the rocky shore.

By the time he had reached a point that he estimated to be halfway, the subtle ocean breeze grew into intense and short-lived gusts of wind. Michael decided to take a short rest before proceeding to the mountaintop. He sat down and winced at the strange feeling in his stomach. It wasn't pain, but something very uncomfortable. He shrugged the feeling off with pure willpower and let his eyes rest on the blue ocean some distance away.

The sight of the ocean gave him some solace. The waves that he had so often gazed hitting the shoreline with force were now small peaceful forms far below. Somehow, the whole ocean seemed very still in the distance, even though its surface was filled with waves that must have been at least one meter high. The power of perspective was tangible. It filled Michael with the familiar inner peace for a short moment. However, the moment made way for the desire to reach the mountaintop. He quickly estimated how many miles he had walked so far and what lay ahead. Rationalizing the situation devoured the fleeting sensation of peace. Soon, Michael found himself again strolling along the Craven's Path, counting the steps as he slowly proceeded to the destination.

He had seen no one else after departing from the cabin. The memory of the villagers' friendly smiles unveiled some longing for human intimacy. The landlord's last words echoed in his mind with the rhythm of his steps. 'Beware the loose stones when you arrive near the top. The Craven's Path isn't so easy anymore in the last few hundred feet,' the man had warned. Michael remembered to heed the warning.

His waving thoughts kept him company the whole way up. Sometimes, they would produce frustration because he knew how long a walk there was ahead of him.

At times, he would feel victorious for even coming so far on the mountain. Some parts of his walk went by on fast-forward, and Michael found himself a great distance from where he was last aware. Thoughts had a strange power on his steps and his proceeding. It was evident that he wasn't present at those times. Most of the walk, he was somewhere else, slumbering under the surface of a waving sea.

After a half an hour of climbing, the path grew rapidly steeper. Michael found himself breathing heavily. He had to take small breaks every few hundred feet. Then, after climbing over a small and steep rise, his destination opened in front of him as if greeting a weary traveler with a warm smile. The summit was just a ten or fifteen minutes away, or at least that's what Michael thought.

Very quickly, the summit's warm smile began to feel mocking as Michael felt he wasn't approaching it at all. The path was very steep and covered with loose stones that slipped under his feet once in a while. A precipice that opened to the south bordered the path very close. 'The Craven's Path' didn't feel like meant for cravens anymore. In his mind, Michael could see how the wiseguy, who had put up the signpost down below, chuckled at the thought of all the men seeking the easy way up. He had to be careful lest his previous mental images of a broken spine and a cracked skull proved real.

A few times, Michael almost tumbled down. Only his panic solution of throwing himself to lay flat on the path saved him from a perilous situation. After some panic rescues, throbbing bruises appeared in his knees and bleeding scratches covered his palms. Nevertheless, Michael was relentless in his decision to reach the mountaintop. His concentration deepened with every step of the way. Very soon, no thoughts flooded his head anymore. No fear of falling down from the precipice invaded his mind. Worries of not reaching the summit didn't occur to him anymore, and no regret of coming to the mountain passed his thoughts. Death was not present. Not even as a looming shadow. A careful step was followed by another, and another, and his balance felt magnificently controlled. All movements felt full of life—he felt even the tiniest changes of balance in his soles and the gusts of wind in his fingertips.

*The Sacred Moment*, Michael realized and let the short thought fade away on the path he left behind. His awareness of the surroundings burned like the flame of a thousand suns. Time was not present in the Sacred Moment—no expectation or anticipation crossed his path. A simple and peacefully breathing world unfolded within him. He embraced it silently like the precipice greeted the vastness of the empty space opening to the south. Michael's heart pounded in his chest wildly, yet with a steady and soothing rhythm. That rhythm was reflected in every step and every movement.

*The Sacred Moment is revealed when the mind is attuned to the world's rhythm—not trying to resist it*, Michael thought and stopped for a while to take a breath in a steady position. *All my life I've been resisting this rhythm without even knowing it. Have I been afraid of it? Have I been afraid of what might unfold if I let go? If I just flow forward? I've lived a lie—my life was never my own creation, but a consequence of my learned reactions to the world's rhythm. All those years of success underlied by silent suffering have been a product of inner resistance. Oh, this beautiful rhythm. How could I have ever resisted it if I had only felt it?*

Michael's thoughts lingered for a while before they withered into silence. A strong gust of wind wavered his balance, and he had to kneel down on the path to keep his stance steady. The precipice was too near to make any mistakes. The Craven's Path reclaimed its silent message of irony once again. Michael was sure the path must have took some lives over the years. There was no way someone had never fallen down off the precipice.

He climbed further on the path. Slowly his steps regained the rhythm of his heart again. His mind was rendered silent by the rhythm, and the familiar state of stillness unveiled from beyond the thoughts. His breathing felt steady. The wind brought a different smell of the ocean—not damp like down on the shore, but crisp and refreshing. The sun was still scorching hot, and it created an enjoyable balance with the cool air. Michael's short shadow thrown on the rocky path by the high sun almost touched the edge of the precipice. For some reason, he felt comforted that his shadow didn't fall off the cliff. Michael made sure his entire shadow stayed continuously visible.

Suddenly, Michael found himself standing on the summit. He looked around in wonder, trying to calm down his racing heart and fast breathing. Only a few more steps and the ocean would open up before his eyes. Michael wiped some sweat off his forehead and proceeded to take the remaining steps when he realized a curious paradox of the last part of his journey. The experience of time had not been present. Even though Michael had been fully aware of where he was coming from and what his destination was, *time* was not involved in the journey in any way.

*All my fears and all those ideas about the approaching end of 'me'—my death—have been absent,* Michael realized. His feet stopped moving. *The Sacred Moment does not include the experience of time but the awareness of change. Each of my steps was taken with full awareness, compassion, and love, even though they were taken with life-threatening danger. 'I' was not there, even though I was there. Not as a person who had a beginning and an end—'Michael, the business emperor'—but as something other.*

For a fleeting moment, Michael's sense of identity shattered into billions of pieces. He could almost hear them crash down on the rocky path under his feet. His identity disintegrated in an instant. All that was left was an awareness witnessing the end of the idea of 'Michael', and it felt good. Witnessing himself disappear was the most liberating experience he had ever had. All those faces he had worn over the years turned one by one into dust and were flown far away with the wind. The absence of his myriad faces made space for emptiness to breathe and dance within him. Everything was embraced by that emptiness. Every single thing in his awareness was engulfed by it, including the awareness itself. The emptiness was not expressionless and dead. It teemed with love, compassion, and life. It danced within Michael's heart and all around him, and was swayed by the wind and illuminated by the sun. The emptiness was blessed by the awareness witnessing it. It danced and danced like there was no end to it.

Michael had no idea how long he stood there. When the mystical experience disappeared as abruptly as it had arrived, he found himself smiling. He realized that he had not *really* smiled for many of those long years of his success, not until arriving at the village and meeting Old Man. Not until now. All those conditioned smiles given in his life of empty success felt meaningless compared to this one. This smile lit up his face and heart for no reason at all. It was unconditional and felt like a blessing.

*Echoes of the Sacred Moment*, Michael thought and remained standing there for some time, just smiling and breathing with his eyes closed. The strange feeling in his stomach had increased during the last part of the climb. Still, the feeling was secondary and compassionately embraced by the smile on his face. Some pain was present, but it didn't matter to him. Not at this moment. The pain waved in and out, like the gusts of wind came and went. The pain's nature was ephemeral, but the smile on his face remained.

Michael proceeded the last steps of his journey to the mountaintop. He was greeted with a breathtaking view of the open sea down below. He took deep breaths of the refreshing air and let his eyes rest on the scenery. The village was seen in the distance, and he could almost swear there was a fleeting sense of the fish market's smell in the wind. Then his eyes wandered along the shore, and he saw the coconut tree grove. Far away, it looked minuscule. Some large areas of white sand covered the rocky ocean floor in front of the grove. The trees were still and blended perfectly with the shore surrounding them. Michael was sure Old Man was sitting under one of those trees right now, smiling the same smile that lifted the world's weight off Michael's heart. The smile he shared with Old Man felt like a protective spell cast on the world, even though there seemed to be nothing from which he had to protect himself. The need to survive was no longer present. Its absence surrounded him with a silent sacredness.

"All thoughts are restricted by time, and time is nothing save the limit of our knowledge," Michael said aloud to himself when the idea appeared in his mind. He then continued with a short thought: *And all knowledge is so small compared to this.* The smile widened on his face. He could swear those were Old Man's words. Maybe Michael, the dying business emperor, was gradually being replaced by someone—or something—a lot wiser.

Michael put down his backpack and sat down on a big rock that was comfortably warmed by the sun. He took a sip of water that had also been turned warm in the scorching sun, but nevertheless, it tasted good after the physical strain of climbing up the Craven's Path. As he put the bottle back down, he noticed his notebook in the backpack. Michael must have forgotten it there while packing for the day's journey. Then, for no reason at all, he took the notebook and a pencil in his hands and started writing.

He wrote for several hours, one sentence at a time, then gazing a long time at the vast blue ocean below and then returning again to writing. He sat there on the big rock in silence, without any intentions or plans on what he should write. He wrote only because he needed to do so. Not once did he stop to read what he had written. When he put the notebook back in his backpack, he had only a vague idea of the message it withheld. Still, the idea nourished the smile on his face for a long time before returning back toward the village.

# THE DANCER

The memory of the trip to the mountain was the only thing keeping Michael barely on the positive side of things. The warm embrace of the Sacred Moment still occasionally calmed his restless heart. Still, it wasn't nearly enough to keep the dark thoughts from arising. There was a strange irony in the high experiences on the mountaintop leading to the emotional descend back to the cabin. He felt more imprisoned by the past than ever. The knowledge of the slowly but steadily waning future loomed in the dark corners of his mind. Michael had some vague idea that he was walking through a personal Hell like the story's warrior had done. However, the idea didn't save him from the suffering the Hell produced.

On the same evening that he had returned from the mountain, a high fever had taken hold of him. For three days and nights, it ravaged his weakening body. At some point, Michael was sure the end was now near. Still, like a rebellious, independent entity, the body eventually started showing signs of healing. The first sign was the painkillers producing even some effect and lowering the fever to a more manageable level. Despite the times of relief, he felt uncertainty within his heart—the fever was most likely caused by the strain of climbing the mountain in his weakening physical condition.

The landlord proved to be a savior of a man during the long hours of disease. He supplied Michael with water and freshly cooked fish from the fish market every day. The man was wary of staying for too long in the cabin in fear of contagious fever, but still, he delivered the water and fish right next to Michael's bed. It was at those times, during the short human contact and a few words changed, that Michael most strongly felt the memory of the Sacred Moment in his heart. But very soon after the landlord had taken off, the loneliness would creep in, accompanied by its dear friend fear. *Maybe my condition has developed more rapidly than the doctors expected*, Michael found himself thinking over and over again. No matter how much he resisted, the thought always came back like a record player on repeat. The uncertainty was literally trying to kill him. On a few occasions, he hoped it would, but the stubborn body would not give in.

After a few days of fever, the short periods of slight relief turned to more extended and more stable periods of painkiller-induced comfort. Such comfort was definitely light at the end of the tunnel. The light was just the opposite way of what he had thought in the darkest moments of this particular Hell. This light pointed to the doorway into life rather than the end of everything. Eventually, Michael started to eagerly wait for his next visit to the coconut tree grove. He would tell Old Man everything he had experienced on the mountaintop. He played with the idea in every way, trying to find the correct words he would say to Old Man. Michael was sure Old Man already knew everything he had to say, but nevertheless, he would have to say it all. After all, he had found the truth of the Sacred Moment. The knowledge of it shouldn't remain only his own.

One morning, when the first rays of the sun were just about to greet the new day, Michael decided to head to the grove. He was still weary from the week-long disease, but his decisiveness was relentless. The memory of the Sacred Moment burned bright within his mind. It whispered him not to linger anymore. Without eating breakfast, Michael filled the water bottle, grabbed his notebook, and first headed toward the village post office.

While strolling through the streets, the people's familiar and friendly smiles warmed his weary heart. It had not occurred to Michael before how much he had learned to appreciate those genuine smiles and the 'good mornings' he exchanged with the villagers. People he hardly even knew. The streets were filled with long shadows of the rising sun. A light wind whispered its silent words in

Michael's ears, and some birds were dancing high above in the clear sky. Everything was simple. Everything felt easy.

In the post office, Michael put his small notebook in an oversized envelope and made sure it would make its way to the destination. He still couldn't recall clearly what he had written in it, but he felt confident it should be sent on that very morning. It was just as important as meeting with Old Man in the grove that day. With a smile on his face, Michael continued through the village. He stopped for a while in the fish market to feel the familiar atmosphere before proceeding for the grove.

Michael strolled on the beach, slowly heading toward the coconut tree grove. The enjoyment of being alive gradually arose with the morning sun ever higher. The shadows of existence shortened with every step. He felt tempted by the sea's fresh smell, and for some distance, he walked in the knee-deep water. Despite all his spent time in the village and the beach, this was the first time Michael stepped into the ocean. The water was clear and warm. It caressed his feet with a soft and gentle embrace. He was aware of the same freedom he had felt on the mountaintop. Freedom, which he was just getting to know after the life-long imprisonment of being 'Michael, the business emperor'. Enjoying his freedom, Michael, the dying man, stopped for a while to look back. He gazed at the mountain's distant silhouette. It seemed to smile at him silently, yet with its whole magnificent being.

After the slow journey through the morning, the coconut tree grove opened before him. The grove seemed somehow different—newer and more alive than before. The quiet enjoyment of life that had carried him along the beach lit up as he saw the familiar silhouette of a man under the tree. Michael felt passionate to tell Old Man about the Sacred Moment he had experienced on the mountaintop.

"Michael, you look well," Old Man said and smiled as Michael sat down on his usual spot. Then, he continued abruptly. "There's an ancient saying: 'Those who speak do not know. Those who know do not speak.' This is the paradox in speaking about the Sacred Moment. Therefore, you should choose your words wisely, coming from deep within, or prefer not to say a word."

"How do you…?" The question froze on Michael's lips. Abashed, he couldn't find any other words to fill the void of ideas that suddenly unfolded within him.

"Oh, I'm not clairvoyant, if it crossed your mind." Old Man chuckled. "The whole village talks about the westerner who went up the Craven's Path. And I know from a personal experience that the mountain can have some serious effect on your life's perspective. So, Michael, tell me how was your trip up there?"

"It was…" Michael struggled to find the words and eventually got his thoughts together. "It was liberating. The freedom I experienced there was unrivaled, unlike anything I've ever felt before. And since that, I've been trying to get the experience back. The closest I've got is while walking on the beach today. Still, today was like a faint echo of the power of freedom I felt there. I know it was the Sacred Moment, but I think I lost it in the hands of the fever."

"What makes you think it was the Sacred Moment?" Old Man inquired with an expressionless look on his face. "That it felt magnificently liberating? That you were happy at that moment? That you felt a strong sensation of overcoming yourself? You see, Michael, the Sacred Moment can bring upon such experiences, but don't mistake the experiences for the Sacred Moment. I do not mean to understate your experiences up there. If you investigate the nature of experience carefully, you will find out that all experience is temporal. The nature of experience is to have a beginning and an ending, no matter how powerful it is.

"Whatever is time-bound cannot last forever. What is timeless will live through all beginnings and endings. The Sacred Moment is timeless. Its embrace is prone to create powerful and soothing experiences. Your mind will then try to grasp those experiences, and you must know that the memories cannot bring you the Sacred Moment. This is the egoistic illusion of many seekers of truth—that they themselves can somehow attain the truth."

Old Man paused as if he was trying to find the words. Michael felt they were now treading on a very delicate matter whose balance would be ruined with any redundant weight of words. The grove's silent shadows under the scorching sun breathed carefully and awaited with eagerness what Old Man would say next.

"Truth can be unveiled only when there's no seeker of truth. Otherwise, something very limited is mistaken for the truth. True freedom can be attained only when you relinquish the idea of yourself attaining freedom. Forget yourself and just watch the world unfold. Watch it carefully and attentively. Let truth and freedom arise by themselves without your interference. Let go of all your desperate need for control and desire to have the world one way or another. Then, and only then, you will find freedom—not as an experience, but as your most essential being.

"Your memories of the Sacred Moment point to something charming indeed, but stop chasing the memories. A ray of light can never catch the shadow. Memories might have kept the fires of hope burning during your illness, but they will only take you so far. Hope is illusory when it relies on any kind of past or future. Don't try to get back what you had then because those experiences do not exist anymore. Memories will only give you explanations. Don't follow your mind and egoistic desires into them. And remember that all explanations of the world are only vehicles for understanding that the world doesn't need explanations. Time is only a stepping stone into timeless."

"I see," Michael uttered and felt like laughing. After a short moment of silence, he spoke softly. "So, my own efforts in getting back the freedom I had on the mountain were actually the only thing keeping me apart from that freedom? Oh, I've never seen my own mind as I see it now, after these weird conversations with you. When

I really look at it, it's evident how all my desires and actions aim for an ultimate freedom, the natural state of a human being. And I can see the problem introduced by my own mind—I'm trying to find that natural state of freedom from things in the world around me. Hah! My mind has always pointed in the opposite direction from where I wanted to be. It's quite sad, actually. It never occurred to me that on my journey to find liberation, I was the only thing standing in the way of liberation."

"The ego is a sad mechanism of the mind," Old Man said silently. "There's one in every human being unless it is entirely brought into the light of awareness. You must relentlessly track down all paths and go to the very end of your mind. Not through any techniques or psychiatric digging up things, but through whatever arises in the present moment. Only that will expose the ego completely. Remember to just expose and do not change. When you are aware of what you are without trying to change what you are, an inner paradigm shift becomes possible. The light of awareness is the light of change. It will obliterate any shadows of illusions."

"Say, Old Man, there's much talk about ego in the world where I come from, but what, actually, is the ego?" Michael tossed the question in the air spontaneously.

"Now that's an interesting topic, Michael, which very few stop to scrutinize. Very few, very rarely," Old Man answered and smiled at Michael as a father would smile at his son. "The ego is a false sense of identity. It is a mirage constructed by your mind. The ego adopts many forms in different situations based on your abilities and your feeling of control. In other words, it resembles the mask of your personality. However, the ego is not directly what you call your personality—the ego is identification with personality. When you mistakenly believe that your thoughts and beliefs are true and your feelings are important, a false sense of identity emerges. This has ten thousand symptoms and consequences in human lives. Possibly the worst of them all is the belief that you act without ego.

"Michael, whenever you meet anyone who declares that he has no ego, you better run. Such ones have committed atrocities and started wars. The ego is the need for control, the desire to rectify and protect the truth. The ego is the need to survive either in life or a petty battle of opinions. The ego calls for more egos to emerge, like a fire that spreads and ravages drylands. It leads you astray into a game of life that you believe must somehow be won, lest there be suffering. In that game, which prevails in the world you come from, life itself is forgotten.

"You see, your personality is actually quite beautiful and unique. Living through your personality is a blessing given by you to you. In case you forget that personality is only a mask and take yourself too seriously, you become unable to take the mask off whenever needed. And to be even more precise, you become unaware that you're wearing a mask.

"Ultimately, the ego presents everything that you are not. Acknowledge its presence in you. See the ego as it is and be aware of all the consequences it has in your life. You can never transcend something that you're not aware of. Awareness, Michael. Awareness, awareness, and awareness."

Michael's mind wandered to his past life. Ego was spread all over the imagery. His life as a business emperor had indeed been a game that had to be won and survived. The news of his approaching death had brought great suffering because of the blind desire to survive. His life as a dying man had not been easy at first, but it had opened entirely new doors of perception. Earlier, Michael had heard some words of wisdom about how one had to die during this life to become a new person, change habits, and achieve great things. But facing a real death revealed the emptiness of those words. The inevitable presence of death had caused a paradigm shift in his mind, which his mind would have been unable to produce before.

The wordless wonder of his ego-ridden past had time to sink in as Michael gazed quietly at the slowly waving ocean. The waves rolled peacefully ever onwards, arriving from the unknown horizons only to merge with the vastness of the ocean. Up and down they moved, like a dancer following a steady rhythm. Michael's awareness wandered from wave to wave as they appeared and disappeared. Occasionally, he glimpsed at Old Man's unmoving profile in the shadow of the tree. Old Man had the familiar expressionless look in his eyes, relaxedly fixed on something unseen that lingered beyond the distant horizon. The silence was deep in the coconut tree grove.

The sun made its way over the arch of the sky. The shadows of the coconut trees grew shorter and changed their direction to grow longer again. The peace that emanated from the grove's wordless silence overwhelmed Michael as it came and went like the waves of the ocean. He needed nothing just sitting there. The feeling of being liberated from his own desires was the greatest liberation of all. He didn't ask for it, nor did he seek it. Liberation simply was there, all-encompassing and powerfully silent.

"Michael, your mind can offer you only a horizon—the limit of your sight," Old Man broke the silence. "Leave the mind as it is and sail with the winds of awareness to see what lies beyond the horizon. You will find out the most beautiful symphony is played there now and forever. Beyond the horizon, the temple bells peal out neverending, calmly and lovingly. There, just one step beyond the sight of your mind, the formless dance of emptiness creates forms. When I was a young boy, I heard a piece of wisdom which I didn't truly understand for many long years. I regarded it as a nice parable only. Still, for some reason, the parable came back to me like those waves arrive at the shore—relentlessly and neverending. Time after time, I heard it from the mouths of different people. I had always understood it intellectually until the time came that I had to lay my intellectual arrogance aside. A time of immense suffering—an indescribable personal Hell."

Michael stayed silent. A tear ran down Old Man's wrinkly face. There was no effort at all to suppress the pain of an untold memory. Old Man took a couple of deep and wavering breaths. Somehow, Michael felt that his own personal Hell—the death of Michael, the business emperor—was nothing compared to the pain radiating from Old Man's shadowy figure. This pain had to have something to do with losing a thing more precious than one's own life. Despite the obviously painful moment, the peace that emanated from the old eyes never broke, not even once. The peace was steady and constant, like an exhalation that never wore out.

"It was a time of transformation. Time of letting go. Personal Hells are always difficult to walk through, but I see it now as a shift of life within life despite the painful memories. A change of posture in the dance of life. Life's strange beauty can be seen in the pain also if you're but willing to see." Old Man wiped the solitary tear from his cheek and smiled. "Michael, have you ever considered the possibility that life was not supposed to make you happy, but instead, to shake you awake? That your whole spectrum of suffering, no matter how deep and devastating, was actually a blessing? Suffering introduces the possibility to awaken, like stepping off a stair in a dream. First, it startles you. Then, if you give enough attention to what's really happening, you awaken from the dream. When you awaken, you find out that despite the pain, nothing is wrong anymore."

"No. I must confess I've never looked at suffering that way." Michael knew the wisdom in Old Man's words but had never experienced it. That grain of wisdom created a small explosion of ideas in his mind. "I've grown up to think that suffering is bad. I've always felt it must be expelled with force because suffering makes your life unbearable. Modern society forces a thought in your head that you must always thrive. If even a small grain of suffering emerges in your life, you must instantly strive to make your life better. And if you don't try, you are considered weak and somehow inferior—not directly, but unconsciously by other people through disguises of compassion and what appears as love. And when you suffer, you are the one who most aggressively attacks yourself. Not a direct attack, but if I've learned anything from my time here, the mind works in very ambiguous ways. Living with suffering is not tolerated, neither personally nor collectively. I guess this idea has its roots in the human desire to not experience suffering.

"Maybe people feel compassion for those who suffer because of their own desire to get rid of suffering? Now that I think of it, it's quite selfish and actually resembles more fear than true compassion. Fleeing from suffering is in our nature. Modern society has done nothing but empowered this desire. I'm not saying we should not try to find a way to cure suffering in the world. If I've learned anything here, I suppose that instead of dealing reactively with the outside world, we would do well if we first turn our attention within to see what's really driving our actions. Maybe this way, our actions would not beget as much predicament in the world as it has in the history of mankind?"

"Asking questions and turning within is always a good choice before acting. Yet, remember that things are never as black and white as our thoughts and words describe. There's always a hidden depth beyond them." Old Man improved his posture to emphasize the importance of his words. "Michael, pay full attention now, as this might be one of the most important things words can ever convey. Understanding this parable, which I heard as a young boy, creates depth beyond the words and thoughts.

"Some mystics have said that God dances the world. Now, there cannot be a dance without a dancer. They are intimately connected in a mutual arising. If the dancer stops, the dance stops. When the dance continues, the dancer appears. The dance includes many forms— different kinds of steps, a variety of moves, constant shifting of balance, and drama. The dance tells a story in which drama is in the details. Every single move is important to carry out the whole performance. They are all needed. It is easy to look at the dance and get lost in the myriad forms, thinking about all the previous moves and anticipating what will happen next. Those forms create the most compelling emotions, coloring the way the dance appears. In the middle of this all, the dancer itself is not seen anymore. Confusion arises.

"Now, it might sound weird and far-fetched that you see the dance but do not recognize the dancer. Yet, this is exactly what happens when you forget your own essence and start believing in your thoughts. This phenomenon occurs when you go looking for God. The vast majority of the human race are looking for their gods and their truths, each one in their own way. Only a few of us notice that when you really look at the dance, then the possibility of recognizing the dancer arises. Just look at the dance—not the ideas, memories, and expectations. Bury all thoughts. Bury yourself as the thinker of thoughts. Give undivided attention. Observe the creation while remaining silent within. Then, the creator will appear. Let reality unfold. Then, God's peace will smile upon you."

Old Man paused for a while, not so much looking for words but letting the words come out when they became ready. Michael found himself gazing at the ocean with only one thought repeating in his mind: *'When a song of a bird breaks the silence of the sea, watch closely, and you will see the dancer in the waves.'* The villagers' old saying brought up a passing memory of the temple and the bells. Some longing and warm feelings accompanied the memory. After a while of lingering in the memory, all his thoughts disappeared.

"What this parable indicates is that you are the heart of the dance and the soul of the dancer. No one else and nothing else. Without you being aware of it all, there wouldn't be a dance," Old Man continued. "The ego in you sees this impossible because it feels separated from the rest of the world, but the essence in you knows this as the truth because it is one with everything. Your choice is always and forever whether to follow the ego's illusion of separation or be the essence of the performance. This is the fundamental communication between the dance, dancer, and observer—whether to step in the world of forms or be formless. If you choose the forms, your life is a neverending dance of pleasures and sufferings. If you choose the formless, you will find out the dancer is you, and the dance will fluctuate between wisdom and love.

”True wisdom originates from the emptiness inside. The deepest love emerges from the oneness outside. The idea of the dance and the dancer resonates with you because you already bear wisdom and love within your essential being. This essence is the root of love, acceptance, and gratefulness. Everything originates from that same essence, only appearing in different forms, like gold, which can form a ten thousand jewels but is always gold in essence. Everything is golden, Michael. Everything.”

"How come I don't see it always that way—that everything's golden?" Michael blurted out before realizing that the question, and the thought behind the question, were ultimately meaningless. He already knew deep within the answer but still continued the questioning. "Where does the essence go once in a while? Especially in my past life, I certainly didn't always perceive everything as golden. I saw jewels, but no gold. There were much silent suffering and stress involved. Much seeking and trying to acquire peace in the best way I knew, which I suppose every human being is unconsciously doing. Why do we forget the essence so easily?”

"There's no direct answer to your inquiry, Michael. Yet, I will give you a direction which to follow.

Be relentlessly aware of following it, lest you end up astray." Old Man chuckled in his curious manner. "Find out how the ego in you operates and affects your life. Do not deny its existence, and do not seek to change it nor the actions it produces. Instead, enlighten your actions. When the illusions of the ego's night are brought into daylight, your deeper self will start to awaken. This will happen in time, maybe when you have suffered enough. When it happens, you will find out that time has nothing to do with realizing the essence.

"The essence is eternal, and the closest approximation of eternity is *now*. Here and now is all that exists, and what exists is eternal. You cannot be apart from it even though you sometimes forget it. Michael, place your trust in this. Reality seeps to existence through myriad forms—human beings, animals, plant life, inanimate objects, happenings, experiences, and thoughts. You can appreciate them and be grateful for them. Yet, the forms themselves are not reality. If you try to find reality from them, you will impose suffering on yourself. Find out what lays beyond the forms here and now, no distance away from yourself. There, you will find something the mind cannot understand. Something deep and again deep."

The familiar deep silence fell on the coconut tree grove. Michael and Old Man both sat there motionless, gazing at the horizon. Slowly the sun made its way down, painting immensely beautiful colors in the darkening sky. Michael felt silence deep within. No ideas of 'Michael, the

business emperor', or 'Michael, the dying man', interfered
with his presence. Everything was peaceful. All was well.

# The Cigarette Shop

Again, one week had gone quickly by without a glimpse of Old Man in the grove. Michael went there every morning to sit and relax for some time. Occasionally, the grove's peace embraced him, and he just sat there under his tree, watching the ocean's endless waving in inner silence. Sometimes, he would wait for Old Man to appear. Michael thought of the conversations they had in the previous weeks and the conversations that would happen if Old Man came. Still, every morning, the coconut tree grove was found empty.

One morning, after an uninterrupted and good night's sleep, when the sun was about to rise, Michael decided to break his routines by taking another route to the grove. He took his water bottle and started up the road, which led to the Craven's Path. Some distance before arriving at the crossroads, where the solitary signpost stood, he changed direction. He headed to the other side of the village.

There was no path, and the terrain proved to be difficult. Michael climbed over small hills one after another. Some of them were covered in long green grass and smooth to walk. Others had loose rocks hidden under the grass. After a few times almost spraining his ankle, Michael decided to take his shoes off. The loose rocks didn't tip his balance so easily while barefoot. At some places, treading barefoot felt uncomfortable with dried grass and gravel pressing against his soles. Still, the uncomfortable sensations made him feel more alive, grounded and aligned with nature. He decided to continue barefoot.

After a while of proceeding through the rugged terrain, Michael arrived on top of a small hill. He gazed at the village in front of him and saw it from an entirely new perspective than before. The village seemed a lot bigger from there. In the distance, some fishermen were returning from the sea to bring fresh fish to the market. The streets were becoming gradually more crowded as the villagers started their morning routines. Some faint sounds of people chatting were carried to his ears by the light breeze, but he couldn't make out any words of it. The sun had just risen entirely to cast long shadows of the people in the streets. The mountain smiled with its majestic silence behind him.

It had been exactly three months since the doctors gave Michael three months to live. Yet, he felt great. He had not been in such an excellent physical condition for a long time. A dramatic change in diet and daily walking had done something close to miracles in a couple of months. A passing thought of the looming death crossed his mind. For a while, it felt conflicting with the aliveness of his body. The thought disappeared, and Michael was left standing on the hill in serenity. A subtle opening into the peace he had experienced in the grove was present. He embraced it gratefully.

The fish market was starting to get crowded. Michael decided to head through the village on his way to the grove. Some distance away from the fish market, he noticed that he had forgotten the shoes on the hill. Still, walking barefoot felt so vivid and magnificently uncomfortable that he decided to get his shoes back later. The smell of the fish had become very familiar, and Michael didn't care about it anymore. The villagers were as smiling as always. Many good-mornings were exchanged while walking through the crowd. It had been a long time since he walked through that side of the fish market.

"Good morning, Michael," a familiar hoarse voice said behind him. "May I walk with you?"

Michael was startled. He had never met Old Man anywhere else, but the coconut tree grove. "Oh, sure." Was all that he came up as he turned. Old Man had just come out of the cigarette store. To Michael's surprise, he placed a 'closed' sign on the door. Without locking the door, Old Man smiled at Michael and started walking with him through the market.

"Very slowly now, Michael. I'm an old man with weary feet." Old Man chuckled as they made their way through the crowd.

Michael walked slowly, as instructed. He felt confused by the radical change in the atmosphere. The villagers did not exchange good-mornings anymore when they walked by. It was as if Michael and Old Man moved in an invisible sphere of silence, a few feet wide, inside of which deep silence prevailed in clear contrast with the outside murmur of the crowd. The silence was not awkward, though. It was full of appreciation, gratitude, and other nameless peaceful feelings. Warm smiles surrounded Michael and Old Man while they slowly proceeded toward the shore. Some villagers put their palms together as if forming a silent prayer. Some bowed down as a greeting—just enough to show appreciation and not too down to be mistaken for a bow for authority. The fish market was soon left behind. The crowd's murmur continued as if nothing extraordinary had happened. They strolled just as slowly on the shore toward the coconut tree grove.

"No wonder why I haven't seen you in the grove for a while. This pace will take us forever to get there." Michael couldn't think of anything else to say. Old Man laughed shortly, yet sincerely, at the joke. Questions were storming in Michael's mind. "So, you own the cigarette store?"

"I do take care of it." Old Man smiled, gazing at the ocean as they walked. "You cannot actually own anything in this world. Everything's passing, but there are some times and places where you're bestowed a possibility to take care of something or someone. I do take care of the cigarette store. It gives enough income to sustain the body—to earn my food and a humble shelter to spend my nights. Additionally, this village is filled with people with warm hearts and caring attitudes. What else does a man need?"

"I guess not much," Michael pondered. In his previous life as a business emperor, it literally had never occurred to him that a human being didn't actually need those profits he'd always been after. Of course, profits bore the potential for doing many good things, but that hadn't been the first motivation in being 'Michael, the business emperor'—success and recognition were. "You don't seem like a cigarette store caretaker. Are you a smoker yourself?"

"Occasionally. Sometimes," Old Man said, and as if he had guessed the hidden idea behind Michael's question, he continued. "Smoking is bad for health, I've been told. Yet, what is life without some small pleasures? Many pleasures are in conflict with your ideas of perfection. However, you don't need to become perfect. Life doesn't need you become a polished human being without any vices to bear. You might have noticed that life always includes vices and virtues. Whether you embrace one or the other, ultimately, it doesn't matter. What matters is your awareness of who you are and what you do.

In the wake of awareness arise acceptance, gratitude, compassion, and forgiveness. As a result of those, something which seems like perfection may arise, or it may not. Let perfection be if it is. Don't crave for it. Ultimately, you don't know what perfection is—it exists only as an idea in your mind. Therefore, forgive yourself for trying to become perfect.

"Reaching any level of perfection will not provide you with the love you desire. For the ego, it is very difficult to be enough to be loved. Sometimes even impossible. Forgive yourself for feeling that you're not enough. Therefore, you can occasionally smoke whenever you feel like it. This little imperfection, just like any level of perfection, will soon pass and vanish in time. Michael, be grateful for your imperfections for the time being, no matter how destructive they are. If anything can be trusted in the realm of time, it is that very shortly, your life will shift. All the imperfections and perfections will change to something else. And if you're truly aware, this shift has already started taking place."

"What if someone else does me wrong? What if you sell me a cigarette, and I start smoking and end up dead because of lung cancer. What about forgiveness, then?" Michael felt the urge to investigate forgiveness further. He had never thought of it as much, but now that Old Man brought the topic up, it switched on Michael's interest.

"Why would you not forgive him?" Old Man glanced at Michael. "Forgiveness is not something that must be earned—not by anyone or even yourself.

Forgiveness is an aspect of your essential nature. It is one of the expressions of your essential being. There's no reason why you shouldn't forgive someone else, other than your own thoughts of the situation. Whenever you don't feel like forgiving, you're embraced by mind-made fear. You fear that if you forgive, you will release the other from responsibility. If that happens, who's responsible then? You are. But you're afraid to be responsible. You're afraid to admit that no one else but you made your life happen. You're afraid of yourself. Only when you truly forgive everything unconditionally will you release your fear of yourself."

Old Man kept his slow walking pace in silence. In the distance, the coconut tree grove opened up to greet the sea with its ever-present peace. Michael awaited eagerly to sit under his tree, listening more to Old Man's words.

"Michael, I've never told this to anyone, but I feel the story must be shared now," Old Man continued after a while. "I've experienced war. It was a long time ago when I was a young man. I had a family back then—a beautiful wife, three even more beautiful daughters, and one beloved son. It happened, that before the war even properly started, the invaders came to our small village. They burned everything down and murdered everyone except young men. We were sent to a prison camp to do heavy physical work. That early morning, before the sun arose, I lost everything. My life became a portrait of pure suffering and incredibly painful emptiness. For some years in the prison camp, this suffering deepened and deepened. I recall trying to take my own life a few times, failing miserably in it.

"In the beginning, there were a few thousand of us in the camp, but when the war ended, only nineteen of us walked out. When I came out, something had shifted within me. The suffering had burned a hole so deep in me that there was nothing else to burn anymore. Who I was before was no more. Walking through those gates into freedom, I could hear the symphony of the bells loud and clear. I realized something very fundamental. During my time in the prison camp, I had been in real danger. Not in danger of losing my life, which I had already lost, but I was in danger of losing my compassion for the invaders. There had been anger, hate, rage, and many dark personal Hells during those years. Yet, the moment I walked out, I realized that I had forgiven everything they had done.

"The young man who had agonized on the smoking ruins of love forever lost—the man who experienced the Hells of war, torture, and loss—had died in those dark cells. Counterintuitively, his death was not the end of everything, but true liberation. This realization was a stepping stone into life, which now produces these words to you, Michael. And don't get it wrong—the memories of those times still remain, often accompanied by many tears. I would give everything to have my family back, and the easiness of life we had before the war. Yet, what unfolded through that young man's death, has since looked everything with endless compassion and forgiveness."

"I'm sorry, Old Man. So, you're spiritually awakened, then, as people say?" Michael tossed the abrupt question in the air spontaneously, trying to avoid the painful topic of loss. "Is this kind of compassion and forgiveness possible to us all, or just some chosen few, like you? At least, I haven't heard the sound of the bells since my dream. Not even a little chime."

"Remember the story of the man and the mountaintop?" Old Man smiled compassionately. The smile brought back the deep wrinkles in his face. "Don't take anyone's word for what anything is. I'm just a traveler, telling my own story. You must find out yourself what it means to be, as people say, spiritually awakened. However, here comes a piece of powerful advice. If a thought 'I'm spiritually awakened' ever crosses your mind, and you go about telling that to other people, then most probably you are nowhere near spiritual awakening.

"Ultimately, there's no spiritual awakening at all—there's no one to awaken. When you realize this, there's no Michael to whom the realization happens. Only the realization emerges. The words and their meanings are only pointers. If you go about seeking advice on how to awaken spiritually, be very careful. When someone tells you that some kind of an awakening is the end of all suffering, the mind will reactively try to find ways to end suffering. This leads only to a deepening of suffering. Don't follow your mind on this, but find out what suffering is. Turn every rock around to uncover who is the one who suffers. This you can do only by accepting your suffering, no matter how deep and hurtful it is. This is part of the journey that you must travel alone. No other traveler can help you with this. They have their own journeys to find out exactly the same what you're set to find out."

"This sounds like a mountaintop paradox." Michael laughed shortly. "Everyone's approaching the same summit, eventually getting there. Yet, there's no path which to follow besides what I'm following at the moment. And this 'I' applies to everyone. No one has paved the way, and no one leaves any footprints. All I have is an old man telling me that there is a mountaintop. The rest I have to figure out myself."

"Maybe you have some hope after all." Old Man smiled at Michael. "Never chain the bird to the ground to save it from falling. The bird's nature is to fly, and the winds will carry her to the mountaintop. The fish does not survive breathing air, but the underwater currents will take him to the soothing depths of the ocean. Just let all the birds and fish be as they are. Turn within. From within yourself, you will find the guidance needed. When you can hear the guidance—the pealing out of the temple bells—you can look upon all the birds and fish with compassion and forgiveness because they cannot stand in your way. All they want also is to reach the summit.

"And here's another mountaintop paradox. When you reach the summit, it becomes evident that you never actually left. The whole journey down and back up was something quite meaningless as if it had not happened at all. Seeking something called 'awakening' and trying to end all suffering is like searching for a way to the mountaintop while standing there. You are already here and now, on the brink of oneness and unity."

They walked the rest of the way in silence. After some time, Michael and Old Man arrived at the coconut tree grove. Michael sat down under his tree, but Old Man remained standing, gazing at the ocean with the familiar expressionless look on his face. For a while, no words were needed. The grove's peace embraced them both. Then Old Man improved his posture, still standing, and faced Michael.

"Michael, some time ago, I underwent surgery. Exactly three months ago, the doctors gave me three months to live," Old Man said with a silent voice. Before Michael could say anything, Old Man continued. "A few days after that, I felt a calling to come here, to this coconut tree grove. I've never been here before, even though I've spent quite a many years in this village. The sound of the bells has been with me since walking out of the prison camp's gates. Yet, in this grove, the symphony is always amplified magnificently. All this time with you here has been an answer to the calling I felt. I've walked with you up to this point. Now you must continue alone from here. Go within, Michael. Be relentless and turn your attention within, no matter what waves of thoughts and emotions will follow. My legacy has been passed to you through words. I'm ready now. I'm ready to go now.

"Oh, and by the way, I've done everything needed to ensure that the cigarette store is now yours. You're the new CEO of a small empire."

Old Man's face was a portrait of compassion. His eyes shone with pure forgiveness and love as he turned back to where they had just come from. Michael wasn't sure if he had even heard Old Man's last words. He felt the urge to say something and go after Old Man, but some unknown force within him made him stay silent and motionless. An emptiness fell down on the coconut tree grove. It wasn't a soothing and silent kind of emptiness, but one filled with trembling anxiety. Dark feelings that had been absent for some weeks rushed back in, like a tsunami. An intense personal Hell was about to make an entrance in the life of 'Michael, the dying man'.

# The Sound of the Bells

Michael didn't sleep at all during the night. Thoughts of abandonment stormed in his mind. Anxiety choked his chest. *How could Old Man have kept such a secret only to himself? Why didn't he tell me about it earlier? Was it even possible that Old Man had gotten his death sentence from the doctors exactly on the same day as Michael had?* Michael felt uneasiness grow more while thinking all the questions.

Michael felt abandoned and betrayed. Old Man had been his safety and support while walking through Hell. Occasionally, waves of compassion washed over him as he remembered Old Man's story about the war. He could still see the lonely tear on Old Man's cheek in the coconut tree grove. The memory brought tears to Michael's eyes. Then, the compassion turned again to anger and abandonment. 'Michael, the dying man', was left orphan in a world he never made. He was carelessly tossed by life again, just like three months ago.

The morning sun shined through the curtains. Michael was still laying in the bed, staring at the ceiling. The cracks in the ceiling resembled the cracks in his life. One opened to the left, telling a story of loneliness. Another expanded to the right, whispering of an approaching death. The ceiling was threatening him with its inanimate stillness.

*This is it. I've had enough. I'm gonna go back to give last instructions about the empire to Jason. Then, I'm going to crawl to die in the hospital. They have at least proper medicine there,* Michael thought. Somewhere deep within, he realized that he had not thought with such intensity in a long time, but the realization was washed away by a sudden tsunami of frustration. Michael plugged in the charger in his phone. *I'm just gonna jump in the bus and book the next flight back home.*

As soon as the phone went on, all Michael's thoughts ceased. There was no network at all. Michael waited for the phone to charge a few minutes, and then rushed outside. Still no network. He ran to the road leading to the Craven's Path, to get to a higher ground. The phone showed no signs of connection. He changed direction to head to the coconut tree grove.

Michael ran barefoot until he arrived at the grove. There he stopped and collapsed to sit down under his tree. Running barefoot had scratched his feet, and some blood painted his dirty soles. Then, Michael started weeping and laughing at the same time. He couldn't quite figure out what kind of mixed emotions produced the tears and the laughter. *All this time I thought I could easily get out of here if I wanted. All those moments I almost called Jason! And now it happens that it was impossible all the time*, Michael thought.

He flipped the phone a few times in his hand. Then, he stood up, screamed as powerfully as he could, and threw the phone as far in the ocean as he could. With a distant and insignificant splash it disappeared under the gentle waves. Michael sat down again, trying to feel the familiar peace that usually emanated from the grove. He would have given anything to hear even a tiniest sound of the bells from the depths of the ocean. Still, nothing but anxiety and frustration prevailed. He stared at the empty place where Old Man had sit. The emptiness of the grove cast a looming shadow of invisible threat on him. The ocean's small waves arriving at the shore whispered silent words of terror to his ears. He had lost something precious, which he could never get back. The problem was, Michael didn't know what it was. Old Man? The peace of the grove? A promise of a compassionate death? What was it that he had lost, that carved a bleeding hole in his soul?

*Abandoned. Betrayed. Lonely. Fine, if it must be so, I'll die here. I'll end my days here and now. Now is the time the doctors promised me. There's nothing for me in this world anymore*, thoughts echoed in Michael's mind. He leaned back on the trunk of his coconut tree. The tree felt rugged and hard against his skin. He noticed that he had ran all the way to the grove wearing no clothes. A huge wave of shame colored the canvas of anxiety and frustration with dark colors. He tried to stand up, but his feet felt utterly powerless. *Dear life, you beat me. I'm ready. I'm ready now*, Michael thought and simply gave up and let go.

He felt his body relax and his mind slow down. It was as if a mental fist he had been clenching with all his powers was now opened. Through that opening, the trunk of the tree felt more rugged against his skin. The ache in his soles started to feel more vivid and painful. The sun, which was closing on its highest point of the day, almost blinded him with its brightness. The ocean waves whispered neverending tunes in his ears. He could feel the presence of the mountain far behind, shedding its ever-majestic smile upon him. Michael could distinctly feel his heartbeats and the strange tingling in his hands and feet. His breathing relaxed and slowed down.

Despite surrendering and offering himself to death, and contrary to his expectations, Michael found out that the body wasn't actually dying—it was more like attuning. Maybe it wasn't his turn yet, after all. The body was coming to contact with the life energy it bore within. The energy was subtle and indistinct, yet very profound. It came in like the waves of the ocean, accumulating in silent power and depth every time the waves hit the shore of his being. Soon, the energy overwhelmed him. 'Michael, the dying man', who he was at the moment, disappeared under a huge wave without leaving a trace of his existence. Deep silence and peace prevailed for a moment, and then, thoughts concerning Jason and the empire emerged. The thoughts invited another wave of overwhelming energy.

The wave washed away everything that remained of 'Michael, the business emperor'. Then came the turn for 'Michael, the businessman', and 'Michael, the ambitious college student'. 'Michael, the friend, the media person, the lover, the child', and everything that he had ever thought of himself, were completely washed away one by one. Gradually, he diminished into strange emptiness. Nothing remained.

Nothing remained to do anything. *I need do nothing*, was the only thought that echoed in the empty valley of Michael's being before fading away. Time had lost its grip of him—the past and the future ceased to exist since there was no 'Michael, the identity', giving life for the game of causes and effects. Time disappeared with all his identities under the waves of the silent energy. His need for control was entirely relinquished, not by Michael himself, but by the wordless recognition that there was no one to be in control. There never had been.

He smiled. The peace of the grove had come back, more prominent than ever. It embraced his still body and welcomed his empty mind. It greeted his awareness like an old friend after a lifetime of separation. There was nothing spectacular or miraculous in the grove's peace or the strange soothing energy he felt within. They were like valley streams—flowing silently in the depths of his being. The present moment was all there was, not as an experience, but as a flux that had no beginning or end. The sun, the sky, the ocean, the horizon, the trees, and his naked body were all reflections of the awareness of this flux.

Light breeze began to blow from the ocean. The breeze brought something very distant with it. At first, it wasn't anything perceivable, but slowly the sensation started growing. The breeze brought a whisper of something forgotten from the depths of the ocean. A tiny bell chimed once. A long silence followed. Then, the sound of another tiny bell, and another, and another. Soon, the ocean breeze emerged with the majestic sound of great bells, colored by gentle tones of the tiny bells. The bells were pealing out just like in the memory of the distant dream. Their symphony was beautiful. Nothing was needed anymore. The sound of the temple bells was perfect.

The grove was quiet and peaceful. A shadowy figure sat motionless under one of the biggest trees.

# The Notebook

The dream was a strange one. Jason woke up sweaty, the echoes of the bells still ringing in his ears. He lay down on the office couch where he had spent three nights in a row. Jason saw no reason to go home since there was much work to do and many meetings to attend that week. Luckily, no one was awaiting him back home. The office had all the luxuries his home had, so the decision to turn the office into his base camp had been quite easy. Jason covered his ears to get rid of the bells that still pealed out through the memory of the strange dream.

"Jason. Are you there?" Mia, his secretary, knocked on the door. "It's you daily mail, and you have fifty two new emails in your inbox. We need to go through the plans for your day."

Jason was tired. Too tired to answer at first. He rubbed his eyes, still lying on the couch, and stared at the scenery in the huge office windows. The city opened in front of him. The morning was still early, yet the streets were already teeming with the headlights of the cars. The lights of a chopper appeared from behind a scryscraper in the distance and soon disappeared behind another scryscraper. The city was awaking to a brand new day of hustle and fuss. Once upon a time, the view had been magnificent. He had gazed at it with awe, but now the work was much more important than spending time with a scenery. Jason was now responsible for the empire that Michael had abruptly left for him.

"Morning. Come in," Jason said, welcoming Mia with a forced smile. "How was your night?"

"Better than yours, I guess. At least, I got to sleep in a proper bed." Mia smiled warmly back at him while walking straight to the desk in front of the window. She placed some papers and a notebook on the desk, sorting them very carefully for Jason to go easily through. "Not much of these papery things anymore. Your real job awaits in the inbox. Oh, and one thing here. Someone has sent you a notebook in mail. I didn't dare open it. It seemed personal, but here it is on your desk also. Want some breakfast?"

"No thanks," Jason replied, stretching as he got up. "Some coffee would be nice, though."

Mia smiled and nodded, and left the room quietly. There would be some coffee soon to get the day running. Jason strolled slowly to his desk to check the papers. One by one he quickly went through them, and piled them on the left side of his huge desk. The notebook was the last item. Jason opened the notebook and his heart instantly skipped a few beats. He collapsed on his chair and for a fleeting moment forgot how to breathe. The notebook was Michael's.

"Mia!" Jason shouted after getting hold of himself. Mia appeared after a few long seconds with a questioning look in her eyes. "Mia, where did this notebook come from? Did you check who sent it?"

"I'm sorry, I don't know. It came in a rugged giant envelope in the morning mail and the envelope is already disposed of. Usually, the mail content answers your question," Mia answered, clearly confused.

"Usually, it does," Jason whispered and covered his face in his palms.

"Everything ok, Jason?" Mia took an uncertain step closer.

"Actually, I don't know yet," Jason answered, perplexed about the whole situation. Something within him wanted to scream, to rectify things, to retaliate for Michael's inconsiderate decisions. After three months, Jason had finally gotten hold of his new role as the CEO of the empire. Everything proceeded as planned. All had been stabilized at last after Michael's disappearance. Now, the man had the nerve to interfere after months of total silence. And with a rugged notebook. He could have given a call at least.

"Let's find out. I'll call you if I need anything," Jason said to Mia, stood up and walked to the couch. Mia nodded silently and left the room.

Jason sat down on the couch. His palms were sweaty. His thoughts were racing in every possible direction, obviously trying to find a way out of the stressful situation. Yet, there was only one thing that could lead out of it. Jason opened the notebook.

~

Jason,

I'm writing this to you on a mountaintop. Literally. The view here is quite amazing, much like the view in your office window. The scenery is a bit different here, but both views share the same magnificence.

I have no idea why I'm sending this notebook to you. There's no hidden agenda in this. To be honest, I don't even know what these pages will contain after I'm done. In fact, I haven't got the slightest clue. Yet, I feel compelled to write. One thing I know, though. Whatever words follow from now on are meant just as much for me as they are for you. So, let's get straight to the point, whatever it turns out to be.

Business equals people who try to find ways to make their visions real. There's nothing wrong with that. Many visions in this world are beneficial to present and future generations. However, as the case almost always is, with the human mind in the picture, things tend to become more or less distorted. It happened for me silently and surreptitiously. Reflecting my past business life, I've led a life of quiet desperation. Silent suffering followed me like a shadow everywhere I went. I wasn't even aware of it back then. I thought I was making visions and dreams into reality, but all I truly had was history turning into nightmares. And the thing about nightmares is that you're not aware of a dream being a nightmare until it becomes evident, until certain happenings tell you so. Business can be a madhouse, and as you *really* look at it, it most often is. When you play by the rules of that madhouse, you become a prisoner in a straitjacket.

Jason, I encourage you to find a way to matter, not by becoming rich and famous, not by adhering to the general rules of the madhouse, but becoming unlimitedly compassionate and caring. If you're not truly caring, your business will crumble down in the sad graveyard of temporary mechanics and numbers. And remember, don't seek meanings from what you do. Not even meanings of compassion or caring. The idea of achievement intrinsically holds meanings within, unless consciously removed. Meanings entangle you, suffocate and pull you down into the chains of your personal history—chains that other people have forged for you. There's always a vested interest in meanings, whether you see it or not. You can make the lives of the people you touch better, and I hope you do, but don't become attached to the idea of making things better.

*Better* will happen by itself when you do what you do wholeheartedly. And as you really contemplate it, you can't even know what is better and what is worse. You don't know *perfect*, but only your personal perception of perfection. Now, that is insanely limited, wouldn't you say? What is a perfect world? What is a perfect human being? What is perfect life? Defining any vision as *perfect* creates delusions of righteousness and justified wars. And all justified wars have their victims. Jason, drop perfection, and instead, commit to whatever you do *here and now* with your heart and compassion. Enlighten the present moment with your attention.

If all the people were like you and I have been—chasing a vision after another—the whole planet would have crumbled to dust a long time ago. Progress, as we understand it in modern society, is a devouring idea, a mechanism of destruction. True progress has nothing to do with technological or economical advancement. This kind of advancement can be beneficial in many ways, of course, but only if we don't interfere with it through our distorted visions of perfection.

Believe it or not, advancement will happen just as likely without our personal interference. Existence grows and holds an intrinsic will to blossom. Just look at flowers and forests—despite moments of suffering and death, there's life and beauty all around. This is hard for a thinking mind to accept, but if you give it even a tiny bit of true attention, you'll find out it's true. The only difference is, when we don't interfere with progress through our personal biasses, things evolve naturally. The human mind has a strong tendency to practice things in excess, to attach illusory dramatic meanings to life. This makes the natural balance of being and doing tip solely on the side of compulsive doing—the science of achievement, instead of the art of fulfillment.

The curse and madness of the modern world are *ignorance* and *want*. For example, nowadays, technological advancements seem to connect humanity globally. Yet, is it really connecting us with each other, connecting who we essentially are? Does it truly satisfy our natural craving for connection? As you really look at it, the connection between human *beings* is easily mistaken for a connection between human *self-images*. I've come to realize that all self-images are profoundly illusory, which have nothing to do with who we are. Many seemingly advanced things in modern society are based on self-images and their ten thousand projections. There's much talk about awareness in the wake of these projections, but I don't see awareness. I see ignorance.

This ignorance leads us to want things, to build our self-image into ever more perfect and dramatic proportions. We are so immersed in having the fruits of our actions that it blinds us. Our *want* entangles us in a future we think is somehow more enticing, more fulfilling than this very moment. Our *want* makes our idea of progress twisted and sick. We so easily end up competing with our brothers and sisters, trying to outdo them in any viable way—levels of success, practices, traditions, ideologies, nationalities, religions, you name it. We have lowered ourselves to a vain game of inferiority and superiority. In this game, those of us who act without mental positions, without aiming for rewards and the fruits of their actions, are considered somehow faulty. Outsiders. Yet, those are the ones who are truly powerful beings.

Jason, here comes probably the most important part of my scribbles. You might not accept this at first, but I encourage you to contemplate this. The strange *game of life* is not about achieving something, but simply to be aware of what is happening. Without awareness, ignorance blossoms. Where ignorance roams, *want* grows to sick proportions. I don't mean awareness here as a product of knowledge or psychological activity. I've come to understand that all knowledge and psychological activity is a result of awareness, happening *through* awareness, *in* awareness, and *as* awareness. Awareness is not about thinking the consequences of your actions, for example, how what you eat will transform you, or what you do today will chop down a hundred trees in the rain forests. This kind of knowledge that is bound in time, knowledge of cause and effect, is most often an expression of ignorance, where you have forgotten *yourself*. Of course, knowledge is important also to address, but without awareness, it easily becomes degenerative. So, what I mean by awareness is your *awareness of being*.

True progress is the ability to turn within, to tune your awareness on the channel of *being*. This is something you cannot do as a society. This is a road you must travel alone. Any external guidance or knowledge you follow on this road will lead you astray into the deep forests of meanings and mechanisms. Still, after you've traveled this road truly *alone*, it has a huge beneficial impact on our societies and the world globally. This beneficial impact is possible only when acting from a place of fulfillment.

A fulfilling life is where you act without constantly striving for rewards of your actions. You need not become special or important in any way. Fulfillment is never found in future, but always in who you are—in the recognition and compassionate acceptance of yourself. Action that aims for fulfillment is only noise in the chaotic world of men, just dust in the winds of the history of mankind. Action that *expresses* your fulfillment is the closest approximation of perfection you can ever come up with. It echoes throughout ages. It is not always what people expect of you—not always friendly or openly loving, accepting, giving, or serving. It is *you* acting with total awareness of *yourself*, recognizing and remembering *yourself*. I do not mean the historical 'you', the mask of your personality, the bundle of your personal mental positions, opinions, and beliefs. I mean *you*, who you are beyond all your human vices and virtues. Because in yourself, humanity breathes. In who you are, humanity is most beautifully expressed.

As I wrote in the beginning, I'm literally on a mountaintop right now. I've harbored many dark thoughts and emotions lately, each one less venerable than the other. Yet, at this moment, I find out that my present state of fulfillment is not produced by me reaching the mountaintop. This is not an achievement of any kind. This is an expression of honoring and appreciating every single step—including that rollercoaster of dark emotions and thoughts—that I've taken to get here. I realized this just before arriving here at the summit. I had already arrived before I even started my journey. In other words, I never left home.

Jason, my time is getting near. 'Michael, the business emperor' is dying. At this very moment he is completely gone. Otherwise, these words could not appear in this notebook. I have no doubt he will surface again many times and bring more or less suffering with him. I know for certain that when he appears for the last time, his final disappearance will be truly devastating. Still, as my thoughts reach for the visions of that moment now, I know deep within that it's nothing I can't bear. We all must bear our own disappearance at some point, just as we must bear the disappearance of many of our loved ones.

Suffering is always prone to emerge when we have to say goodbye. Yet, the one who looks through the eyes of suffering is so compassionate and loving, that it will ultimately turn the raging flames of suffering into beautiful glowing embers. And all that will be left is the magnificent view of life as it is. Despite moments of darkness and many personal Hells, every single thing holds beauty in itself as it is.

By the way, have you looked at the view in the office window lately? I mean, really *looked* at the view?

~

Jason stood up from the couch. A tear ran down his cheek. It was a tear one would expect after meeting with an old friend after many years of separation. However, that tear wasn't shed for Michael, but for Jason himself. That tear reconnected him with something precious he had forgotten along the way.

Jason took a deep breath and walked to the huge window. His heart was pounding steadily and peacefully. He looked at the view. Another tear appeared on his cheek as the first one dropped down to the floor. A gentle smile decorated Jason's face.

A tiny bell chimed once.

Then, a second time.

Again, and again.

Everything was good.